PENGUIN HA

SAILING

Peter Stuart-Heaton, who first wrote this book in 1947–8 after leaving the Navy, was born in Yorkshire in 1919, and was educated at Charterhouse. After a varied career which included working as a Clerk in the House of Lords, he has settled to a routine of publishing, book distribution, and writing and illustrating books. He has written many books on ships, the sea and sailing. His only grouse in life is that the summer is too short!

His published works include: *Sailing* (1949); *Cruising* (1952); *A History of Yachting* (1955); *The Yachtsman's Vade Mecum* (1961); *Boatcraft* (1963); *Songs Under Sail* (1963); *The Sea Gets Bluer* (1965); *The Sea Gets Greyer* (1966); *So They Want to Learn Sailing* (1966); *Peter Heaton on Sailing* (1967); *Boat* (1969); *Cruising: Sail and Power* (1970); *Make Sail* (1972); *A History of Yachting in Pictures* (1973); *Motor Yachting and Boating* (1973); *The Singlehanders* (1975). Many of his books have been published in Penguins.

PETER HEATON

Sailing

FIFTH EDITION

PENGUIN BOOKS

Penguin Books Ltd, Harmondsworth, Middlesex, England
Penguin Books, 625 Madison Avenue, New York, New York 10022, U.S.A.
Penguin Books Australia Ltd, Ringwood, Victoria, Australia
Penguin Books Canada Ltd, 2801 John Street, Markham, Ontario, Canada L3R 1B4
Penguin Books (N.Z.) Ltd, 182–190 Wairau Road, Auckland 10, New Zealand

—

First published 1949
Reprinted 1950, 1951, 1952, 1954, 1958, 1959, 1961
Second edition 1962
Third edition 1966
Reprinted 1968
Fourth edition 1970
Reprinted 1971, 1974, 1976
Fifth edition 1978

—

—

Made and printed in Great Britain
by C. Nicholls & Company Ltd
Set in Monotype Times

TO JANE

Contents

CONTENTS

*The theory and practice of navigation and pilotage are dealt with in Peter Heaton's books on cruising.

CONTENTS

Plates

Text Illustrations

Various other sketches appear throughout the text.
All the illustrations are by the author.

Foreword

by

Vice-Admiral Sir Geoffrey Blake, K.C.B., D.S.O.

'THE sea is our life' said Lord Jellicoe. That was a long while back but it is true today.

It is therefore a duty, for those who can exercise it, to encourage the young men and women of today to take to the sea wherever and whenever they can. The years which have passed since the war have shown that in spite of great difficulties, the sailing of all kinds of craft and particularly small boats has again become a national recreation. There is no doubt that the instinct and longing to get on the sea is there, but occasionally there is a diffidence in embarking on something you know little about.

This book, which everyone can afford to buy, discusses in simple language and in an attractive form the whole question of choosing, buying, fitting out, and handling a small boat. Experience alone can produce a good seaman, but there is much which can be learned from reading and study.

Reading it myself after sixty years at sea certainly gives me the urge to start all over again. The small sailing boat has been the one which has always appealed to me, although the open sea in a fine seagoing craft is a great adventure.

Peter Heaton has done a good job of work in producing this little book. It should be widely read by those who wish to become seamen, by those who think they are seamen, and by the old hands who know how much there is still to learn. One caution only remains for me to add. You are always up against the elements and largely dependent on them. We cannot control them, thank Heaven, but if you study and respect them, they will respect you.

Geoffrey Blake.

ACKNOWLEDGEMENTS

I wish to acknowledge with gratitude the assistance received from: Vice-Admiral Sir Geoffrey Blake, K.C.B., D.S.O., F. G. G. Carr, Esq., and Maurice Griffiths, Esq., G.C., for their invaluable advice; F. Beken and Sons, Cowes, who supplied the photographs for Plates 1, 6, 8, 9, 13, 14, 15, and 16; and Eileen Ramsay/J. Allan Cash Ltd, London, for Plates, 2, 3, 4, 5, 7, 10, 11, and 12; *Reeds' Nautical Almanack* for permission to reproduce the compass on p. 207; Seeley Service and Co. Ltd, Publishers, for permission to reproduce certain additional lines to the shanties; the late Cuthbert Mason, Esq., for permission to reproduce certain navigational 'Odds and Ends'.

I would like to take this opportunity of thanking all the very many people who have written to me. To answer all the letters personally would require an army of secretaries! Many of the suggestions put forward were most helpful and have gratefully been incorporated in this reprint of the book. Thanks to these friendly critics it is now a better and more comprehensive book. For both the praise and the criticism I am most grateful.

PETER HEATON

CHAPTER 1

What This Book Is All About

—

THERE are few things in the world so fascinating, so rewarding, or so productive of the good in man as the art of sailing. This is an attempt to collect within the pages of one book the basic principles of this art. There are already many such books on the market, and the only reason I have for launching another similar vessel is that I believe that in this book I can perhaps give the novice the broad essentials on which he can base his future learning, for a sum which he can easily afford.

Yet there is another reason; it was Captain Joshua Slocum who said 'The wonderful sea charmed me from the first.' The more I sail, the more I see of the world of water that fascinated Slocum and many thousands of others before and after him, the stronger grows my affection for it, and the greater the enjoyment I derive from it.

This enjoyment I want to share; to pass on. There are hundreds of men alive today who, for as many reasons, are far more fitted than I to write a book of instruction on sailing, but in one thing I am bold enough to think that I can equal them – and that is in my desire to help others to share the happiness I have enjoyed myself. I want to help awaken the dormant instincts that are the result of the centuries of sea tradition that is this country's greatest heritage. John Masefield calls it 'sea fever' and it *is* rather like an incurable disease.

You cannot tell the exact moment you catch it; the infection is gradual. Its symptoms are many and varied, but if, when the sun shines through your office window, you have a vision of sunlit waters and a forest of slender masts continually blotting out the work in front of you, or if, while making conversation to some acquaintance, you find yourself wondering whether that new chain bobstay will be ready, or whether you'll have the sails tanned this year, you've got it and you'll never get rid of it! It might be argued that to want to spread an incurable disease is a curious way in which to benefit mankind, but there is one important point about sea fever: its victims show no desire to recover. They arc happy in their infection and even tend, in their less tolerant moments, to regard those who have not succumbed as outsiders and Philistines!

To Philistine and victim alike I address this book. And although the inadequacy of a 'handbook' on sailing seems to me to be rather on a par with those books on art that try to communicate the genius in a painting by Botticelli to the man in the street, yet there *are* a number of things which the beginner can learn from a book, and I am bold enough to hope that even experienced seamen will find something in these pages to while away a rainy afternoon. To assist me in my task I have had the advantage of the best advice and resources obtainable, people whose wisdom and experience have only been equalled by their generosity in putting their knowledge at my disposal. The sea breeds generosity; moreover, there is always danger round the corner at sea and danger brings out the finest qualities in human beings, and it is for these reasons that the friendships made on the sea are amongst the most enduring of all friendships.

Of all things made by man there is nothing so lovely as a sailing boat. No two boats are ever alike although they may come from the same builder and be built to the same plans. Sailing teaches self-confidence and humility, initiative and philosophy, it teaches you to be courageous and to take infinite pains. At one moment it calls for courage and determination and cool judgement as you do battle with wind and sea, and the next, lying in harbour or ghosting through a calm, it brings a peace of mind beyond the understanding of landsmen.

If this book helps but one person to feel 'the call of the running tide',* I have succeeded a little in my task. For the rest, once the disease is caught, I have tried to set out in understandable form some of the answers to all the questions that the new victim will want to ask: How to buy a boat? What sort of a boat to buy? Where to keep it? These questions I have tried to answer – but how inadequate must all books be! You can never learn all about sailing. You can never learn all about it even if you live to be a hundred years old. But you can start, and you can start with this book.

So let's get aboard and make sail and when the wind comes and the sails fill, we will hear the creaking of the ropes and feel the boat heeling and will know, with that curious feeling of excitement that is never diminished by familiarity, that a new voyage has begun ...

* From 'Sea Fever' by John Masefield.

CHAPTER 2

Choosing a Boat

—

WHAT sort of a boat? This depends mainly on two things. The locality in which you will be sailing; and the amount you want to spend.

For example: if you live on the east coast and will be doing the majority of your sailing in east coast waters, you should choose a boat that is able to take the ground easily, and which has a centreboard that can be pulled up when sailing in shallow water, thus reducing the vessel's draught. If, on the other hand, you will be sailing on the south coast, you will do better with a keel boat. If you are a west country man the local west country design will suit you. If you are intending to make reasonably long cruises you will need a totally different type of craft than if your aim is sheltered water, class racing. The best thing you can do is *ask the advice of a sailing friend*. Tell him the sort of sailing you propose to do – ditch crawling, coastal cruising, racing in dinghies, etc. – and how much money you want to spend.

Of course every sailing man has his own pet theories, and you should not accept everything your friend tells you as the last word on the subject, but there is no better way of learning how, where, and when to buy a yacht than to ask a man who owns one and is in touch with sailing matters. Another good thing you can do is to join the local yacht club. Here you will get a mass of advice and you will probably get bewildered. But you will be able to 'talk sailing' and benefit by the mistakes and successes of others. There are always lots of boats for sale and many of them are quite useless. The best safeguard for a beginner is to take a sailing friend along, but mind that he knows what he is talking about! If you cannot find such a friend, the following should be of help:

The size of your craft will largely be determined by your pocket. There are many types, ranging from dinghies and open or half-decked boats with retractable keels, to fixed-keel boats, suitable for racing, or cruising boats with accommodation so that you can live on board. Due to inflation, prices are high today, but there are always second-hand boats advertised for sale in the yachting periodicals. You will notice that sometimes a yacht is referred to as a '5-tonner' or, say, as '5 tons T.M.'. This is a reference to an old formula, which is still useful to indicate size, and which can be worked out as follows:

When L=length *on deck* from the fore side of the stem to the after side of the stern post, and B=the extreme beam:

$$\frac{(L-B) \times B \times \frac{1}{2}B}{94} = \text{Thames Tonnage}$$

There are certain basic principles of design which should be known. Firstly, most ships are about three times as long as they are broad; by length I mean the length of the ship on the Load Water Line (L.W.L.). Secondly, the draught of a ship, unless she is a centreboard craft, will be about one-fifth of the L.W.L. The following table is an extract from Uffa Fox's fascinating book *Sailing, Seamanship and Yacht Construction*. It shows the approximate proportions for a given L.W.L.

L.W.L.	20 ft	24 ft	27 ft	32 ft
Beam	7 ft	8 ft	9 ft	10.5 ft
Draught	4 ft	4.8 ft	5.5 ft	6.5 ft
Displacement	2 tons	4.5 tons	8.5 tons	11 tons
Sail area	300 sq. ft	475 sq. ft	630 sq. ft	900 sq. ft

The Displacement Tonnage of a ship is the amount of water displaced by her, and is thus her actual weight, as opposed to the Thames Measurement Tonnage.

Nowadays yachts tend to more beam, but a major development is found in the profile or side-view. The rudder, which used to be a moveable extension of the keel, is now usually separate from it, being hung on its own right aft, sometimes having a skeg ahead of it. These two types of profile are shown in Figs. 1 and 2, which illustrate a number of small yachts of a type commonly found today. Yachts used to be planked in wood. Now most of them are built of glass-reinforced plastic (G.R.P.) or cold-moulded wood, or glass fibre foam sandwich or light alloy. Larger vessels are built of high tensile steel and concrete construction is another newcomer. But the majority of modern small cruisers are G.R.P. Keels may be retractable or not, single or double fin, or (as in some of the boats in Figs. 1 and 2) with a more traditional long keel. Rudders are sometimes hung right aft on the transom.

If you want to race your boat you will find that cruising yachts (and ocean racers) compete against each other by using a rating indicating their speed potential (and their size). This is the International Offshore Rule (I.O.R.). Sometimes advertisements for yachts for sale give this rating, sometimes they give the Thames Measurement Tonnage and sometimes just a few measurements, like length, beam and draught. In Fig. 2b is shown the deck and cockpit of a small cruiser. Fig. 2a illustrates types of dinghy and multihull, while Fig. 2c shows the typical living accommodation of a small cruiser. An alternative would be: two quarterberths right aft, the galley opposite a chart table and, forward of the saloon, W.C. and lockers, and stowage space in the fo'c'sle. The shape of the hull affects the accommodation plan. As you come to learn about boats you will begin to recognize points. One vessel you will mark badly while another you will know with pleasing certainty to be well balanced, good to windward, yet safe in a blow. Talk over with that invaluable sailing friend the kind of boat you think would suit you, whether it be a cruiser, a three-quarter decked centre-boarder or one of the great variety of modern dinghies which cater for every taste and pocket, not to mention the twin-hulled catamarans, wonderfully fast and exciting craft! The really important thing is, whatever kind of boat you buy, to buy one that is a good shape. No matter how much money you spend on her, you will never do any good

Fig. 1 – Nine types of small yacht.

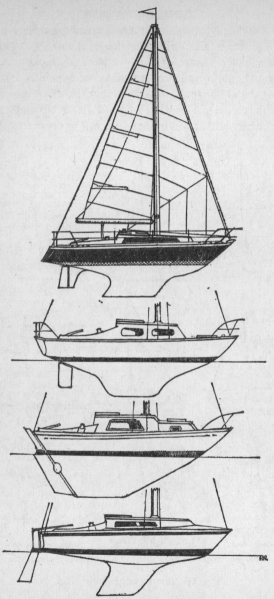

Fig. 2 – Four types of hull.

Round Bilge
Sailing Dinghy

① Centre Board
② C.B. Case
③ Kicking Strap
④ Battens
⑤ Racing Flag

Hard Chine
Sailing Dinghy

⑥ Dagger Board
⑦ D.B. Case

⑧ Retractable
Rudder Blade
⑨ Chine

Racing
Catamaran
[Twin Hulls]

Cruising
Catamaran

'Cat' Bows on

" Deck plan →

View into
Sailing Dinghy

Pulling Dinghies
← G.R.P.
Inflatable

Sculling
Notch

Chock for
Outboard Clamp

⑩ Jib Sheet
Fairlead
⑪ Tiller
& Extension

Fig. 2a – Pulling and sailing dinghies and catamarans.

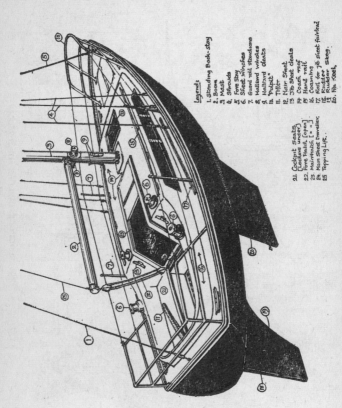

Legend:

1. Standing Back-stay
2. Boom
3. Mast
4. Shrouds
5. Fore Stay
6. Sheet Winches
7. Guard rail stanchions
8. Halliard winches
9. Halliard cleats
10. "Pulpit"
11. Tiller
12. Main Sheet
13. Jib Sheet cleats
14. Coach roof
15. Hand rail
16. Coaming
17. Rail for jib sheet fairlead
18. Rudder
19. Rudder skeg
20. Fin Keel

21. Cockpit seats [Lockers under]
22. Fore Hatch [open]
23. Main Hatch [" "]
24. Main Sheet Traveller
25. Topping-Lift.

Fig. 26 – Cockpit and deck of a small yacht.

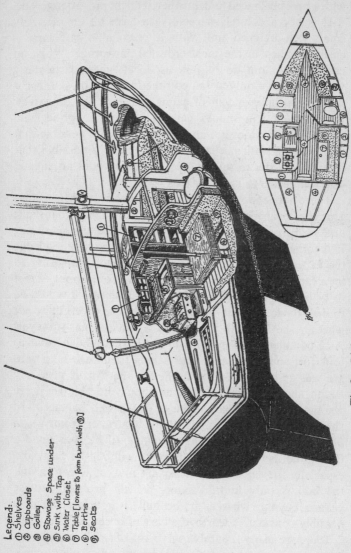

Legend:
① Shelves
② Cupboards
③ Galley
④ Stowage Space under
⑤ Sink with Tap
⑥ Water Closet
⑦ Table [lowers to form bunk with ⑨]
⑧ Berths
⑨ Seats

Fig. 2c – Living accommodation of a small yacht.

with a badly balanced hull. Further, it might prove dangerous.

It is not absolutely necessary to have an engine. Any small well-designed hull with a reasonable sail area is easily handled in the most crowded anchorage. While an engine is without doubt very useful at times, particularly when you have only a limited time in which to sail, for it makes you independent of calms and, to a certain extent, of tides, yet you should never turn down a good boat because she has not got an engine. It is quite possible that you could install one later on, and equally possible that after sailing the vessel for a year or so without an engine, you will decide to keep her that way.

There is one most important point about buying a boat. Have her properly surveyed. It is quite amazing what paint and varnish will do to an old vessel. There are many pitfalls for the unwary, and even if you have some knowledge the experience of the professional surveyor will bring to light faults the ordinary man will miss. You cannot expect to be able to survey the yacht yourself; in fact it would be foolish to do so; but you can inspect her carefully to see whether she is worth the cost of a professional surveyor. As a complete novice, you will not have any idea what to look for, and here again your sailing friend can help you. He will be able to tell you whether the ship is generally sound and not strained and he should be able to judge whether she is a freak shape or looks well balanced. In short he will be able to say, 'This boat *is* or *is not worth having surveyed.*' He will also examine (if he is as good a friend and as thorough as I hope he will be) the gear, and especially the sails. If the latter are absolutely rotten and the hull is only in fair shape, he will probably advise against buying; whereas if the hull is first-class, he may possibly consider it worth the cost of a new suit of sails.

There are many reputable surveyors of small craft. While their reports give no guarantee, they are an excellent guide to the vessel's condition, and well worth the expenditure. A large proportion of the vessels on the market are not worth buying. Once dry rot has attacked a ship it is never certain that the germ has been cured. Old ships can be painted and puttied to look like new, and such things as nail sickness (when the galvanizing has worn off iron fastenings and the iron is rusting and leaving brown stains that may one day start rot) can be concealed from the

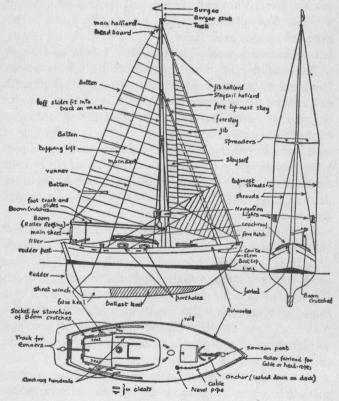

Fig. 3 – Parts of a small cutter.

General Dimensions – L.O.A. 26 feet, L.W.L. 23 feet, Beam 8 feet, Draft 4′ 6″. Sail area 450 square feet. Thames Tonnage 5.

inexperienced buyer by a last minute touch of paint. You can also have your boat surveyed by Lloyds. The basic cost of a survey is not high, unless they open the ship up, removing the ceiling (not the roof, but the planking that lines the interior of a vessel; see 'Parts of the ship') and taking samples of all suspicious parts of the vessel for inspection. It is the cost of putting all this back that makes such a survey rather more expensive. On the other hand it is obviously a very thorough survey, and furthermore you can get your boat classed, which gives an indication of her expected time of useful life.

I have heard people say that they intend to take up sailing, and that they want a very small boat to learn with. It is a fallacy that if a boat is very small it is either easier to sail or safer than a larger one. A very small boat, like, for example, a 12-foot dinghy, is so quick in its response to the helm, and so easily capsized, that it is a very tricky type of boat for a beginner. The ideal craft is about 4 to 5 tons yacht measurement with a moderate sail area. In this the beginner will have time to think, and moreover, if he does get caught in a blow, the vessel will be large enough to take care of herself and of him.

If you intend to sail in shoal waters the following points should be borne in mind when looking for a boat. Choose a vessel designed and built in the locality if possible. If you cannot do this, make sure that the centreboard is properly fitted. A great deal of information on C.B. craft is contained in a charming and useful book called *Everyman's Yachting* (London, Hutchinson) by Maurice Griffiths, former editor of the *Yachting Monthly*, who is one of the foremost authorities on C.B. craft.

Finally, don't be in a hurry. You will have to make many fruitless journeys, and spend quite a lot of money on railway fares before you find the right boat. Good boats are scarce but they are worth waiting for. It is very tempting, after a long journey, to gloss over the bad points and see only the good ones of the craft you have come to inspect. The owner will no doubt tell you of the 'other chap' who is very keen to buy. If you are not quite sure, take my advice and let the 'other chap' (if he really exists) have her. The right boat is there for you if you persevere. Don't think though that any boat is perfect (except in her owner's eyes – the next worst thing to insulting a man's wife is to run down his ship). All boats are a compromise. The hull may be what you want, the accommodation perfect, but the rig may be very old-fashioned and the gear heavy. She may be a beautiful-looking racing type with a lofty Bermudan mast and the manners of a thoroughbred, and yet have practically no accommodation whatever. It is up to you to decide what you want and to weigh up the advantages against the disadvantages.

Remember that the buyer has the upper hand. The man selling is keen to sell. You as the buyer can make him an offer. He has to decide whether he will get a better offer or whether to accept it. If he does not accept it he may have lost his opportunity of a sale. On the other hand, *you* can try somewhere else. There are as good fish in the sea as ever came out of it. So approach the subject with your eyes open. If you like the look of the vessel, and she measures up to your requirements, get your sailing friend to examine her as I have indicated earlier in this chapter. If she appears to be sound, make an offer *subject to survey*. It will be possible that you have heard of the vessel through one of the many yacht-broking firms. In this case, you should make your offer through them and pay 10 per cent of the agreed price to the agent as proof of your good faith, and to give you the legal option on the vessel. Get in touch with a surveyor, who will no doubt agree to survey at the earliest convenient date. The vessel must be hauled out and slipped, if this is not already done, so that the surveyor may examine the bottom, and have one or more keel bolts drawn for inspection. The cost of hauling out will be yours. If the survey report is good on the whole except for some minor faults, you can approach the seller again and suggest that he puts these faults right at his expense. If he is a reasonable man, he will do this. If the survey report is very bad you are under no liability to buy, and have merely incurred the expense of hauling out. Hauling out even a small cabin yacht costs money. As for surveying, the charge varies depending on value, distance the surveyor has to travel, complexity of the survey, and so on. So you *could* find yourself paying anything from £35 upwards for the whole job. Quite a deal of money you will say, and rightly, but you are about to invest considerably more in the boat, and one should no more grudge paying for a good survey of a boat than one does in the case of a house. Moreover, if a friend with reasonable experience has examined the vessel carefully first, the chances of its being hopeless are fairly small, while the surveyor, by finding certain faults which you can then bring to the owner's notice, adjusting your offer accordingly, will be well worth the money spent. Either way it is worth it. And even if there are no faults at all, it is a good feeling to know that you have had an expert to examine the ship. A further point is that if later you should want to sell, it is always useful to have a surveyor's report.

Treat all second-hand craft (and new craft for that matter) with suspicion until they are proved sound. Your relationship with an owner should be like that of a millionaire to an adventuress – courteous but careful!

CHAPTER 3

The Parts of the Ship

—

WHEN you eventually buy a boat, examine her carefully from stem to stern. Postpone the sailing of her until you know more about her. Notice where the lines (ropes) lead. Find the bilge pump and make sure it works. Examine the ballast. See just where it is placed and how much of it there is. Examine the anchor and cable. Find the compass. Is there a foghorn aboard? A boat hook? Navigation lights? Are all the sails there and are they in clean, strong sail-bags? You must know the names of all the various parts and fittings of the ship, and know their functions before you can really understand the later chapters of this book and know what is really going on. This chapter will help you to acquire this knowledge.

Nowadays boats may be built of many materials: wood, plywood, steel, fibreglass, etc. The construction of yachts in plastic reinforced with fibreglass, although comparatively new, is now the most popular method. This form of construction possesses a number of advantages, which will be discussed later in this chapter. I was tempted to leave out the part which explains the construction of a traditional wooden-built yacht, but on reflection I have kept it. There are still hundreds of second-hand wooden yachts in excellent condition. Moreover they are still built, and quite a few people prefer them.

To start with the hull (see Fig. 4). This is the body of the boat. It is built on a long, heavy piece of wood called the keel; attached to the bottom of the keel is another piece of wood called the false keel. Above the keel is another

DESIGN FOR LIVING

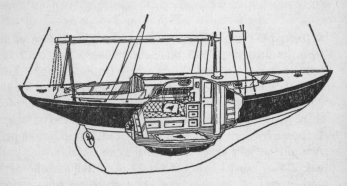

When buying a yacht, consider first her condition
and sailing qualities, but do not forget to examine carefully her layout below decks. Has she
headroom, sufficient lockers, good berths, hanging space? Proper sail stowage? Is her engine
installed in a sensible place? Has she a water-
closet, and does it work? Is her cable locker
adequate, or does the cable stow on the lee bunk?
If she is as snug as the little 8-tonner shown here,
there's not a lot wrong with her!

piece of wood called the keelson. Extending out from the keel on either side are the timbers. Over these timbers are fastened the planks. Now these planks may be fastened to the timbers in three different ways: clinker or clench building, carvel building, and diagonal building.

In clinker-built boats the planks overlap one another and are clenched on to the timbers. In carvel-built boats the planks are laid edge to edge. The edges meet in a V shape with the widest part of the V outboard. This is filled

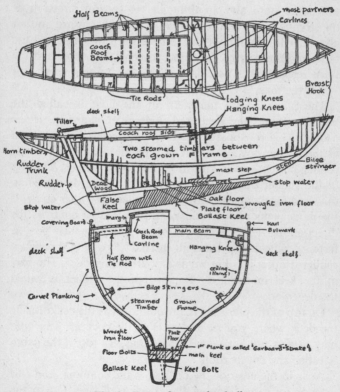

Fig. 4 – Parts of a wooden hull.

with material known as caulking cotton. A stopping is put on top of that and the whole tightened down. This caulking keeps the hull watertight.

Diagonal-built boats have two skins, the planking of the inner skin running diagonally across the hull in the opposite direction to the planking of the outer skin. These boats, like clinker-built boats, do not require to be caulked.

The front end of the boat is called the bow, and anything in the general direction of the bow is known as fore or forward, pronounced 'for'ard'. The back of the boat is called the stern and anything in the general direction of the stern is called 'aft' or 'after'. The terms for'ard and aft also refer to the part of the ship between the mast and the bow, and the part of the ship between the cockpit and the stern respectively. You do not say 'aft of the mast', but 'abaft the mast'.

The plank across the stern of the boat is called the transom. Abaft the keel, and underneath the boat, is the rudder. This is a board which is attached to a rod known as the rudder post. The part of the hull through which the rudder post passes is known as the rudder trunk. The top of the rudder post is called the rudder head. Fastened to this, and extending forward, is the tiller. The tiller controls the movements of the rudder, and the rudder controls the direction in which the boat sails. If the rudder post is fastened outside the transom instead of passing through a rudder trunk it is is known as an outboard rudder. The part of the keel immediately forward of the rudder is called the deadwood.

On top of the planking is a roof known as the deck. Inside the deck where you sit and steer is the cockpit. The boat may or may not have a cabin; if it has, the top of the cabin is called the coach roof.

Around the edge of the cockpit is the coaming, and this extends forward, forming the coach roof side. On to the coach roof side the coach roof is built. It consists of planks running fore and aft fastened on to beams which run at right angles to this planking from one coach roof side to the other. Where the coach roof and/or skylights are built on to the deck the beams are cut down to allow for the space required in the decks, and two stout pieces of wood are fastened at right angles to these half-beams, as they are called. These two pieces running fore and aft are called carlines.

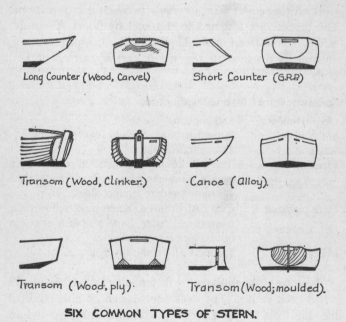

Long Counter (Wood, Carvel.)   Short Counter (G.R.P.)

Transom (Wood, Clinker.)   · Canoe (Alloy).

Transom (Wood, ply).   Transom (Wood; moulded).

SIX COMMON TYPES OF STERN.

Fig. 5 – Sterns.

The foremost part of the bow consists of a strong piece of timber known as the stem. The bow can be straight-stemmed or spoon-shaped with varying amounts of 'over-hang' as the part extending in front over the water is called. A boat can have three main types of stern: transom, canoe, and counter (see Fig. 5). Counter sterns have varying degrees of 'overhang'.

The timbers may consist of grown frames or timbers made from wood which is steamed and bent into the required shape. The planking is fastened to them generally by copper boat nails clenched over roves. In boats of 2 tons or so generally all the timbers are steamed and placed at about 6 ins. apart, but in larger craft it is usual to find two steamed timbers at 6-in. intervals between a grown frame. The timbers are fastened to the keel by floors. These are of oak or iron (see Fig. 4). The ballast keel, which is of lead or iron, is fastened to the wood keel by means of keel bolts.

Some woods used for boatbuilding are:

Grown timbers	Oak, opepe.
Steamed timbers	American elm, wych elm, oak, mansonia.
Keels	Oak, elm, Afzelia.
Planking	Teak, Iroko, mahogany, pitch-pine, Oregon pine, Columbian pine, yellow pine, Marine Ply (glued with resorcinol glue).
Deck planking	Teak, Afrormosia, Kauri pine, yellow pine, western red cedar, Sapelewood, Marine Ply (glued with resorcinol glue).
Masts	Spruce, Californian silver spruce.

The tops of the timbers are fastened to two strong planks called deck shelves. The deck shelves run on either side of the ship from aft right forward. Running also fore and aft and attached to the timbers on the inside of the vessel on either side are the bilge stringers.

To strengthen the vessel, right-angled pieces of oak and/or iron are attached to the main beams either side of the mast. Those which attach the main beams to the timbers are known as hanging knees. Those which attach the beams to the deck shelf are called lodging knees.

The mast has a slot in its lower end which fits into a groove in a stout piece of timber attached to the top of the keel. This is called the mast step.

Yachts are also built in wood using synthetic resin glues, a process known as 'moulding' (either 'hot' or 'cold', the latter being the most commonly found). Cold moulding uses thin wood veneers which are glued in strips. This method produces a light, strong hull, but it has to be expertly done. For amateur building there are good kits of sheet plywood ready cut to shape. These can be glued and screwed together and varnished or painted. It is also possible to buy hulls in wood (and in G.R.P.) for amateur completion; a useful economy if you have the time and just modest carpentry skills, and want a new boat as opposed to a second-hand one. The lightest material for yacht building is aluminium alloy, and it is growing in popularity, though generally for larger yachts. But the most popular method of building today is with glass-reinforced plastics.

So let us take a closer look at this type of construction which has virtually revolutionized boat-building. Although this method of construction is comparatively new, great advances have been made, and new techniques are continually being developed. Probably the most commonly used method is that called the resin/glass laminate method, the laminate being laid up either by hand or by spray. Resin/glass construction gives great strength. Moreover it dispenses with the bogeys of rot and of worm (see Chapter 17). However, before we go further let us just consider for a moment what resin and fibreglass really are.

In boat-moulding a resin called polyester resin is used.

This is originally in the form of a clear, sticky, fluid to which must be added a catalyst to make it set hard. This process of hardening, known as 'curing', takes about a fortnight. During this time various substances are added, the object of which is to make the resin opaque, to strengthen it, and finally to make it the desired colour. So much then for resin. Glass fibre is made of a lot of filaments of spun glass, tiny little filaments, about a ten-thousandth of an inch in thickness.

It is well known that fibreglass may be woven into different sorts of cloth. In the case of boat-building the fibres are cut into short lengths of two or three inches and made into what is termed a 'random mat'. In this 'mat' the strands of fibreglass are arranged higgledy-piggledy to take the strains in all directions. This random mat is enormously strong, glass fibre having a tensile strength comparatively several times greater than steel!

A reinforced plastic boat, then, is built up in a previously prepared mould. Resin glass alone could not have a smooth finish. The finish comes from contact with the mould. The hull is what is known as 'laid up wet' inside the mould, so that the smooth surface of the hull will be to the outside. In hulls of more than 20 feet or so in length, the mould is split longitudinally and the two halves bolted together. The inside of the mould is covered with wax polish so that the hull will not stick to it. A coat of resin is next applied to the mould and allowed to gel. This is followed by a coat of resin into which is laid a ready-made sheet of fibreglass mat. This mat is carefully pressed into every corner of the mould. This process is then repeated with the random mat already mentioned, until the required thickness has been obtained. Next, wooden stringers, ribs, etc. are fixed and moulded in. The ribs are frequently of metal or plastic covered with resin/glass laminate. After this comes the moulding into our hull of thwarts, and gunwale-capping, and, in the case of larger vessels, of wooden bulkheads, pre-moulded cabin top, decks, etc. Our hull is now completed as far as is possible at the moment, and it is allowed to 'set' for about fourteen days.

In the design of craft to be made from reinforced plastic, the yacht designer has the advantage of being able to allow for such things as water and fuel tanks to be moulded into the hull. We have been talking of the resin/glass laminate type of construction, but, as I said earlier, this method of building boats in reinforced plastic is in a state of continual development. A new method finding favour is the 'sandwich' method. This consists of plastic foam slabs reinforced on either side with resin/glass. This method has both buoyancy and great strength.

Yachts may also be constructed of high tensile steel and (a relative newcomer) in reinforced concrete. Let us now consider the spars of our ship.

Firstly the mast. This is a round or oval-shaped vertical pole on which are hoisted the sails. It may be constructed of wood or metal. New yachts will have metal (alloy). The very top of it is called the truck. Where a wooden mast passes through the deck it is strengthened by two pieces of wood wedged between the two main beams called partners. The mast is held firmly by wooden or rubber wedges. The part of the mast between the deck and the step, the part in fact inside the vessel, is called the 'housing' (so also is the inboard part of a bowsprit). The second largest spar is the boom. One end rests against the mast. The metal attachment by which it is secured to the mast from which it pivots is known as the gooseneck. If your boat is gaff-rigged the next largest spar will be the gaff. The top of the sail is laced to the gaff. Over the end of it is a pair of jaws which pass round the mast. In some boats the mast is stepped on deck.

If the boat has a spinnaker, the pole which is used to spread it is called the spinnaker boom. In some boats, a spar extends out from the bow. This is called the bowsprit.

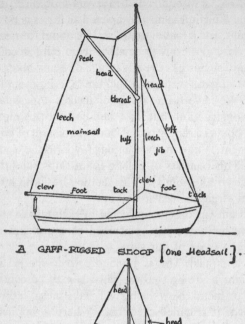

A GAFF-RIGGED SLOOP [One Headsail.].

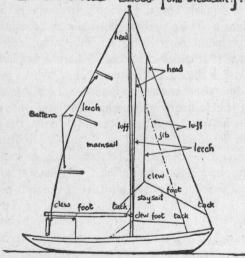

A BERMUDAN CUTTER [Two Headsails.].

Fig. 6 – Parts of the sails.

It is held in position inboard between two stout pieces of oak called knight heads. It has an iron band on the out-board end of it to which are secured the fore-topmast stay and the bobstay (see Rigging). This iron band is called the cranse iron.

Now the sails (see Fig. 6).

Let us assume that your boat is rigged as a Bermudan sloop. You will have two working sails: a large sail, hoisted abaft the mast, known as the mainsail, and a smaller sail hoisted forward of the mast, called the jib.

The forward edge of the mainsail is called the luff, the after edge the leech, and the bottom the foot. The tack is the corner between the foot and the luff, the clew that between the leech and the foot, and the top corner is called the head. The jib is named in the same way. You will probably have another jib, only smaller than the first one. This is the second (or storm) jib and is used when the mainsail is reefed.

The jib is hoisted on the forestay,* a wire running from the bow of the boat up to the forward edge of the mast. It is fastened to this by spring hooks (see Fig. 7).

In the leech of the mainsail are a series of long, narrow pockets. In these are placed thin strips of wood called battens. They help the sail to take up its proper curve.

If your boat has a gaff (four-sided) mainsail, this is laced to the boom and to the gaff and along its forward edge to hoops which slide up and down the mast. The top of the mainsail which is laced to the gaff is called the head. The bottom of the mainsail laced to the boom is called the foot.

* In the days of square-rig, the sails were known by the mast or stay on which they were set. For example: the mainsail was the sail set on the main mast, the fore-staysail was the sail set on the forestay, the topsail that on the top-mast. Nowadays the terms are used some-what more loosely, and in the case of a sloop, although correctly speaking the sail forward of the mast would be the staysail or fore-staysail, it is generally referred to simply as the jib.

The forward edge with the mast hoops is called the luff, and the remaining (after) edge, the leech.

The corner between the luff and the head is known as the throat. The corner between the head and the leech is called the peak. The corner between the luff and the foot is called

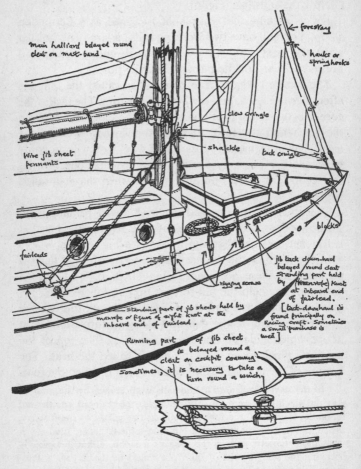

Fig. 7 – The jibsheets (ship is on the port tack).

the tack, and that between the leech and the foot is called the clew. In the four corners of the sail are fastened little brass rings known as cringles. A foot or so above the foot of the sail there is a row of short lines known as reefing points. There are generally three of these rows, each two feet or so above the other. There are cringles in the luff and leech of the sail in line with each of the reefs; they are called the reef cringles. Reefing is more usually done nowadays by rolling the sail (gaff or Bermudan) round the boom (see Chapter 14).

Now the rigging. Rigging is of two kinds, standing rigging and running rigging. The standing rigging is the permanent rigging that supports the mast. The running rigging is the lines, generally of rope, that run through blocks and pulleys.

The standing rigging consists of the following: one or more pairs of shrouds which support the mast on either side of it. In the case of a Bermudan mast, there are generally two sets of shrouds, one set running to the top of the mast and the other set running about half way up it. The upper shrouds are kept away from the mast by means of horizontal struts, usually made of wood, called spreaders. Sometimes there is more than one set of these spreaders; it depends on the height of the mast. These shrouds are attached to the hull by long bands of iron that extend down the sides of the boat either inside or outside the planking. These are the chain plates. The shrouds are attached to the chain plates by means of dead-eyes and lanyards or else, and more usually nowadays, by rigging screws. The lanyards are of hemp, the size depending on the size of the boat. They have more elasticity than rigging screws. Then, running from the bow (or the bowsprit end if there is a bowsprit) to the top of the mast is the fore-topmast stay; and running from the bow (whether there is a bowsprit or not) to a little over half way up the mast is the forestay.

If there is a bowsprit there will be a stay running from its outboard end to the bow, just above the water line. This is called the bobstay.

Then there are two lines that run from a point on the after-side of the mast opposite where the forestay joins it to just abreast the cockpit on either side. These are the runners and they can be hauled on or slackened. When sailing, the windward runner must always be kept taut and the leeward runner must be slackened off.

On most Bermudan craft with their relatively short booms, particularly in ocean racing craft, there is a stay running from the transom to the top of the mast. This is known as the standing backstay.

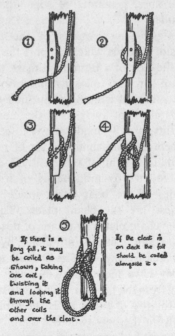

If there is a long fall, it may be coiled as shown, taking one coil, twisting it and looping it through the other coils and over the cleat.

If the cleat is on deck the fall should be coiled alongside it.

Fig. 8 – Belaying round a cleat.

The functions of these stays and shrouds will be discussed in Chapter 15. At present we are just acquiring a vocabulary and identifying the various parts of the ship.

Now let us take the running rigging. The lines with which you hoist the sails are called halliards.* On a gaff-rigged sloop you have three halliards – two on the mainsail and one on the jib. The jib halliard hoists the jib by its head. The two mainsail halliards are called the throat halliard and the peak halliard. The throat halliard hoists the part of the gaff near the mast. The peak halliard is attached to the outboard end of the gaff about two-thirds of the way along it. As can be seen, they hoist the throat and the peak of the mainsail respectively. When hoisted the halliards are held in position by twisting them round a cleat – this is known as belaying (see Fig. 8). Cleats are generally made of wood and are found on the mast and on deck, and often on the sides of the cockpit coaming.

Attached to the clew of the jib are two ropes. One leads to the cockpit on the port side, and one to the starboard. These are the jib sheets. Attached to the outboard end of the boom and running through three or more blocks to give leverage and so to the cockpit, is the main sheet. The sheets are for trimming or altering the set of the sails, by hauling on them or letting them out.

Running from the outboard end of the boom to a sheave or block at the mast-head and down the mast to the deck is the topping lift. It is used to keep up the boom off the deck when the mainsail is not hoisted.

Finally, you will find a selection of miscellaneous gear on board. Firstly there is the anchor. A yacht of any size will have two anchors, one large anchor to which is attached the cable, and one small anchor. The small anchor is used by bending a long stout rope to it. Being light it is easier to pull up than the big anchor, and it is very useful when you have

* Derivation – 'haul yards'.

to anchor for a few hours to wait for the tide to turn when you are becalmed. It is termed the kedge anchor.

The cable consists of a length of chain, in a small boat generally about 25 fathoms. One end is shackled on to the ring of the anchor and the other is fastened (or should be!) inboard. The cable is stored below in the cable locker and runs up to the deck through the navel pipe or chain pipe. There is a metal roller or a fairlead attached to the top of the stem of the boat (the stem-head) through which the cable runs when the anchor has been thrown over the side. Before anchoring you should make sure the cable will run over this roller, otherwise it will chafe the covering board or rail.

To protect your ship when lying alongside another vessel or a quay you should have several fenders or fend-offs. They vary in shape, size, (and price!). Old motor tyres cut in half with a line attached make excellent, if not very beautiful, fenders. If you have bought a second-hand boat, you will probably find, unless you are very lucky, that the running rigging and a number of the accessories need replacing. You will probably also find the following:

A series of very old, cow-tailed lengths of lines that the previous owner thought 'might come in handy some day'; two barely recognizable fend-offs, one in the last stages of decomposition; a whisky bottle (empty) and a primus stove that may some day, somewhere, have cooked something somehow. My advice is; scrap the lot! Start with new gear if you are doubtful whether the old is absolutely sound. It is worth the extra expense to start off with good gear. It gives confidence and pride in one's belongings.

In addition you may find your boat has an engine in it. If this is the case you should do three things. Find the petrol tank and see that the petrol is switched off. Secondly, observe the makers' name and write to them for their handbook on how to run it properly. Thirdly, forget about it until you have learned to sail. You will find it of the greatest use to you later, but you must *never* become dependent on it. Learn to handle your ship under sail first; besides, it is much more fun using your brains to make wind and tide work for you, rather than switching on the engine.

These then are the principal parts. Examine your boat and see if you can identify them. When you know the name of each part you will be well on the way to learning to sail.

RIO GRANDE

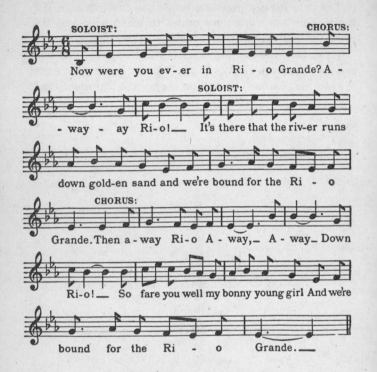

SOLOIST: Now were you ev-er in Ri-o Grande? A-way-ay Ri-o!— CHORUS:

SOLOIST: It's there that the riv-er runs down gold-en sand and we're bound for the Ri-o Grande.

CHORUS: Then a-way Ri-o A-way,— A-way— Down Ri-o!— So fare you well my bonny young girl And we're bound for the Ri-o Grande.—

2.   *'Where are you steering for, my pretty maid?'*
       Chorus: *Away-ay Rio,*
   'And have you a sweetheart, my pretty maid?
    For we're bound for the Rio Grande.'
       Chorus: *And away Rio –* etc.

3.   *'May I stay with you, my pretty maid?'*
       Chorus: *Away-ay, Rio.*
    'I'm afraid you're a bad one, kind sir,' she replied,
    And we're bound for the Rio Grande.
       Chorus: *And away Rio –* etc.

4.   *So it's pack up your sea-chest and get under way.*
      Chorus: *Away-ay Rio.*
      The girls we are leaving will all get our pay,
      And we're bound for the Rio Grande,
      Chorus: *And away Rio –* etc.

5.   *Now fill up your glasses, and say 'Fare you well',*
      Chorus: *Away-ay Rio.*
      To the pretty young lasses who loved you too well,
      For we're bound for the Rio Grande.
      Chorus: *And away Rio –* etc.

6.   *'Good-bye, fare you well, all you girls of the town',*
      Chorus: *Away-ay Rio.*
      And when we come back you may get a new gown,
      And we're off to the Rio Grande,
      Chorus: *And away Rio –* etc.

7.   *We've a jolly good ship and a jolly good crew,*
      Chorus: *And away-ay Rio.*
      We've jolly good mates, and a good skipper too,
      And we're off to the Rio Grande.

      Chorus: *And away-ay Rio,*
              Away-ay Rio;
              So, fare you well, my bonny young girl,
              And we're bound for the Rio Grande.

CHAPTER 4

Moorings

—

WHEN the newcomer to yachting buys a boat he probably has no very clear idea of where he is going to keep her, apart from the fact that nearness to his home is obviously a big consideration.

Let us assume that you have bought a boat at the beginning of the season, and you have bought her while she was laid up in the Isle of Wight. I take the Isle of Wight because the Solent is very suitable for a beginner. There is a fine well-buoyed and sheltered strip of water. There are facilities without number, and when the novice has learnt a bit and wants to be more ambitious, there are many attractive places like Beaulieu, Bembridge, Newtown, Lymington, etc., all within a few hours' sailing distance of each other.

Supposing then that we have bought our boat and she is going to be launched in a week's time. The question is, where shall we moor her?

We can approach the Harbour Master and ask for a mooring to be laid for us in a suitable locality. We can approach a shipyard which has moorings on its frontage that can be rented weekly or monthly. We can rent a berth in one of the new yacht-harbours known as marinas. Or we can put down moorings of our own.

The latter course is not to be recommended for beginners, and indeed it is generally worth the expense of having your moorings laid for you. The local people know the strength and direction of the tide, the direction of the prevailing winds, the nature of the bottom and other important factors. It pays to take local advice on the matter of moorings. It is however useful for the beginner to know how moorings are laid.

Let us consider the primary points to be borne in mind when selecting an anchorage. An anchorage should be in a spot well protected from storms. It should be sheltered from the prevailing wind. Your mooring should not be too near other boats so that your own boat is in danger of hitting them when they swing with the tide and wind.

A boat anchored to a long line will describe the extremity of a large circle. This circle may be made smaller by shortening the line, but your mooring should be in such a place that you can swing quite freely no matter from what direction the wind may blow.

The size of mooring depends a great deal on the depth of water and also on how exposed your position is. The type of mooring it is will depend on the sea bottom. For example, an anchor that will hold well in sand will pull right through a mud bottom, and, vice versa, an anchor that will sink deeply into a mud bottom will slide along on the top of sand.

The most common form of mooring consists of two anchors each with a length of chain called ground chain, to which is joined another length of chain as the riding scope. The anchors should be double the weight of an ordinary anchor, and the ground chain should be six or seven times, and the riding scope twice, the depth at high water; that is, the greatest depth. Get a good, heavy chain. It will outlive a light chain by many years. Even when rusted it has a large factor of safety, and furthermore a heavy chain makes quite a good mooring in itself, and will take much of the strain. Sometimes concrete blocks are used instead of anchors. An approximate weight for a 4-tonner would be $1\frac{3}{4}$ cwt for a single block.

The usual method of attaching the mooring chain to a buoy is to shackle your riding scope to a mooring line –

for example, a 2-inch grass line would be suitable for the mooring line of a 4-tonner – and attach the mooring line to a cork or wooden buoy. This buoy should be painted in a distinctive colour and should have a wire or rope loop on the top of it. It can then be easily picked up.

Where the mooring line is attached to the riding scope the rope will be spliced round a galvanized iron thimble. Where iron touches rope the splice should be protected by a thimble in this way. It is a good idea to have a length of rubber hose on that part of the riding scope which will touch the ship's bows. This will prevent the cable from damaging the paintwork.

To make a boat fast to her mooring, lead the mooring line over the fairlead in the bow and haul in the riding scope. When you have sufficient inboard take two turns round the samson post in the bow of the boat as shown in Fig. 3. This samson post should be well built into the boat and not just screwed to the deck.

While we are on moorings, we can consider the very important subject of anchors and cables. If your boat is a 4-tonner, the minimum weight of anchor you should have is 35 lb. The kedge anchor should weigh about $\frac{3}{4}$ as much as your main anchor. An 8-tonner's main anchor should weigh about 45 lb., a 10-tonner's 55, etc., going up about 10 lb. for every 2 tons. A yacht should always carry two anchors, a large yacht three. The usual amount of cable carried in a 5-ton yacht is 30 fathoms. As you should have at least three times the depth at high water, this means that the greatest depth you could anchor in would be ten fathoms. In practice you will probably often anchor in deeper water, and provided it does not blow up you will be all right. But it is wise to stick to the rule whenever possible. To drag an anchor is costly and unnecessary.

So far when we have spoken of anchors we mean the ordinary fisherman's anchor (see Fig. 9) but the C.Q.R.

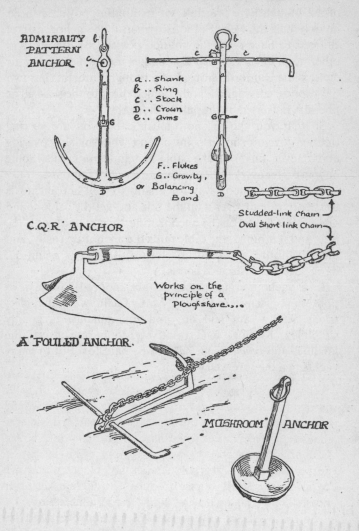

ADMIRALTY PATTERN ANCHOR

a .. shank
b .. Ring
c .. Stock
D .. Crown
e .. arms

F .. Flukes
G .. Gravity, or Balancing Band

Studded-link Chain
Oval Short link Chain

C.Q.R ANCHOR

Works on the principle of a Ploughshare....

A 'FOULED' ANCHOR.

MUSHROOM ANCHOR

Fig. 9 – Anchors and cables.

type of anchor is nowadays much in favour. This makes use
of the ploughshare principle for its holding power. It need
be only half the weight of a fisherman-type anchor, as it is
claimed to have twice the holding power (see Fig. 9). Another good anchor, which also makes use of the same principle, is the Danforth. Instead of a ploughshare, this has two
flat prongs, coming to a point, which dig into the sea-bed as
pressure is exerted by the pull of the cable.

So that you can tell how much cable you are veering
(letting go) you should paint a long white mark (covering
about seven links) on the cable at regular intervals. Some
people prefer every fathom, others every five fathoms.

The most common way for a ship to foul her anchor is
for her to ride up over it on the tide and get the cable round
one of the flukes of the anchor. She then swings with the
tide, and if it blows, the cable pulls the anchor up easily, and
unless you are on board and aware of what is going on,
bang goes that insurance bonus!

In a yacht marina, the boats are moored to quays or
pontoons; often stern to quay. Many facilities – water, elec-
tricity, etc. – are laid on, and maintenance is greatly
simplified. Marinas tend, relatively, to be expensive; the
facilities and convenience have to be paid for. But to many
yachtsmen they are well worth it.

TROUBLE ON AN OCEAN RACE

We beat steadily to windward all evening and by nightfall we could see the Barfleur light on the eastern tip of the Cherbourg Peninsula. The wind had freshened and by midnight it was blowing fairly hard. There should not have been much sea, but we had a foul tide and the tides round this part run fast and kick up a steep sea when they are weather-going. At midnight there was quite a big sea and 'Dinah' was obviously staggering around under too much canvas. We put a reef in the mainsail but we kept the working jib. She was better then, but the wind continued to freshen and at about half past one we decided to tuck in another reef. I accordingly shook Michael, who was endeavouring to sleep. I say endeavouring because none of us had been able to sleep, owing to the water that poured in on top of the bunks. The decks were tongued and grooved and like all small boats' decks they worked a lot when driving hard to windward. The canvas which covered them had rotted in two places, we afterwards discovered, and the water was coming in as if out of a tap. The bedding (we use kapok sleeping bags) was soon saturated. We were, furthermore, taking a lot of water into the cockpit. The helmsman would frequently be blinded by a dollop of spray in the face, while our oilskins were no match for such a determined onslaught by the ocean. But of one thing there was no doubt: 'Dinah' could not only take it but she was going like an express train.

We put the second reef in. It took us much longer than the first. We were all sick, and no one more so than the skipper. Why, in Heaven's name, does one go to sea? Michael went forward to shift the jib and then disaster overtook us. He had got the small jib hanked on, no mean task in that submarine-emulating fo'c'sle, and had got the working jib down when – pang! the starboard jumper-stay parted at the rigging screw. It wrapped itself round everything aloft, making a wonderful job of it. It wormed, parcelled, and served the whole of the top of the mast! Nothing could be hoisted or lowered. We were in a fix! The mast was describing astounding parabolas on the heavens, and in any case with the sail hoisted it was far too difficult to climb. There was nothing we could do about it, and we regretfully decided to give up the race and get her home. With reefed mainsail (we could just carry two reefs) we found she would lay N by E fairly comfortably and we estimated that this would fetch the Nab. It did. At five o'clock on Sunday evening we passed Fort Blockhouse, and tied up on Camper and Nicholson's hospitable moorings.

I suppose sailing people are a little mad. Otherwise why should they voluntarily invite such discomfort? We had had nothing to eat except barley sugar since tea-time on Saturday, being unable to keep anything else within us, and we had been completely wet through for sixteen hours, and yet on Monday morning we were discussing arrangements to enter for the R.O.R.C.'s race to Dinard in two weeks' time. It is certainly beyond the comprehension of landsmen and frequently baffles those who do it. Yet somehow, however hard it may blow and however much one's patience and courage are put to the test, I don't think there is anyone who sails small boats who will not agree that it is worth it over and over again.

CHAPTER 5

Knots and Splicing

—

THE hey-day of the knot was the day of the old square-rigged ships. Then literally hundreds of different knots had to be tied for definite uses. Now alas, many of those old knots have been forgotten and the fascinating art of the rigger is almost lost.

But although the sailor on the small boat needs to know but few knots in comparison, yet when one thinks of knots and splices the mind goes back to those days when sail was in its prime, the days of the old square-riggers. For this reason I have included in this book extracts from some of the old shanties that the sailors used to sing when hauling on the halliards, working the capstan, or pumping ship. Just as the sea and the sailor's art never change, so these songs are as full of tune and vigour today as they were a hundred years ago. All that we learn about the sea is good, and so I have included these old songs in this book on sailing. The verses given show only the repeatable parts of the songs. Many of these songs were bawdy in the extreme, but only the verses. With a strange sense of propriety the sailor kept the chorus, which, being sung by all hands, would be easily heard on shore, from lewdness. The bawdiness was always reserved for the shantyman, quietly singing the verse just for the benefit of the little group round him. There is a similarity between the rollicking bawdy shanty and many of the service songs sung during the last war. Both were expressions of a desire to sing in company, with others doing the same job. But the shanty

was essentially a 'labour song'. It was never sung un-
accompanied by work. But to return to our knots. . . .

All that the beginner need know is how to tie three
principal knots, how to tie a few variations of these knots,
and how to splice. The three principal knots are the reef
knot, the clove hitch, and the bowline.

The reef knot is used to tie in reefs, to tie canvas gaskets
or ropes round the sails for furling, to join two ropes of
similar size together, and for a large variety of other
purposes. It is easy to tie, it will not slip, and what is very
important, it is easy to undo.

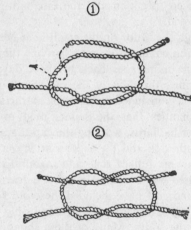

Fig. 10 – The reef knot.

Before commencing to tie this knot memorize the following. The part of a rope which is attached to something
is called the standing part. The end of a rope beyond a
knot is called the fall. A loop formed in a rope is known
as a bight.

Now to tie the reef knot (see Fig. 10):

Hold the rope in your two hands, an end in either hand. Pass the end in your right hand over the end in your left hand. Then pass the end in your left hand over the end in your right hand.

> 'First right over left
> Then left over right.'

A reef knot can be depended upon only when two ends of the same rope or ropes of the same size are tied together. It is not safe to tie a large rope to a small one by means of a reef knot.

Fig. 11 – The clove hitch.

The next knot is the clove hitch. You can use this for mooring to a post or bollard, securing a line to a spar, etc.

Study Fig. 11. Like all good sailors' knots the clove hitch has the twin virtue of tightening under strain and of being very easy to cast off.

Take a post; the leg of an upturned chair will do. Secure one end of the rope. Imagine that this end is now attached to your boat and you are about to secure her to a bollard on the quay side by means of a clove hitch. The end secured is the standing part and the opposite or loose end is the fall.

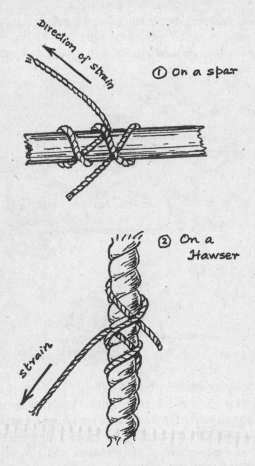

Fig. 12 – The rolling hitch.

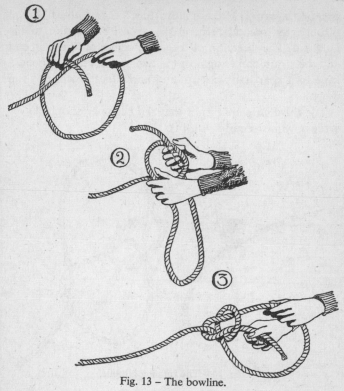

Fig. 13 – The bowline.

Take the rope and pass it round the post, keeping the fall underneath the standing part. Then take hold of the fall and pass another loop over the post, keeping the fall underneath as before. Pull taut and you have a clove hitch. You must remember that it is the strain on the standing part that keeps a clove hitch tight. If there is no strain on the standing part, the knot will not be safe and will slip.

A variation of the clove hitch that will not slip under these circumstances is the rolling hitch (see Fig. 12). Take two turns round, say, a spar; each turn going over the longer end of the rope. Make a third turn passing the free end through the second turn, in the opposite direction to the long end. The direction of the strain comes on the long end and the strain comes against the two turns. You can bend a rope to a spar half way up, and know that it will not slip down.

The third principal knot that the beginner should know is the bowline (see Figs. 13, 14).

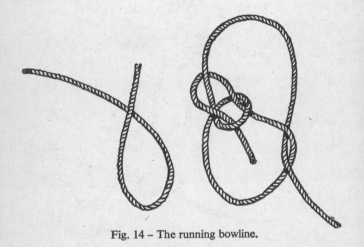

Fig. 14 – The running bowline.

The object of the bowline is simply to make a loop. For example, you can use it to make the kedge warp fast to the kedge anchor, to make fast to a ring-bolt on a quayside, to bend a reefing pennant to the cringle in the leech of the sail, and hundreds of other such uses.

Now to tie the knot. Take your rope and make one end fast to something. That is the standing part. Now, holding the fall in your right hand, place it above the standing part which you hold in your left. Then, without letting go the part held in your left hand, move the left hand higher up on the standing part and form a loop. Notice, at this stage, that you have the loop in your left hand and the fall in your right hand and that the fall goes up through the loop. The standing part is underneath the loop. Finally, pass the fall under and around the standing part and down through the loop and pull tight.

In Fig. 15 we have three other knots which are useful to know. They are all very easy to tie and should be readily

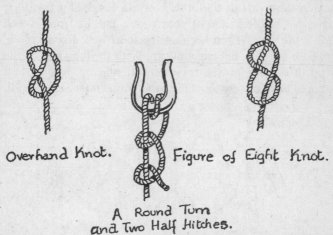

Overhand Knot.   Figure of Eight Knot.

A Round Turn
and Two Half Hitches.

Fig. 15 – Three useful knots.

understood from the diagrams. A round turn and two half hitches is often used for securing a rope to a ring-bolt. The overhand knot is a quickly made knot in the end of a line to prevent it unreeving itself through a block, etc. The figure of eight knot is a development of the overhand knot. It makes a larger knot.

It is also important that you should know how to whip the end of a rope to prevent it from unreeving. There are several methods of doing this, but as in my experience whipping frequently comes off, often at an inconvenient time, I propose to show here how to make a whipping that *will not come off*. It is called the sailmaker's whipping and is made as follows: Take a strand of whipping twine (twine is obtainable from any yacht chandler). Nylon twine is elastic and very strong (see Chapter 15). Untwist the end of the rope you want to whip, for about two inches. You will not need more than a foot and a half to two feet of twine for this job. Now hold the rope's end in the left hand, and taking the twine in the other, form a loop. Slip this loop over the middle strand of your rope's end, and pull it well down the rope. Then keeping the loop well down lay the rope up again as tight as you can. With the long end of the loop of twine whip the rope's end tightly by winding half a dozen or so closely touching turns round it (see Fig. 16(2)).

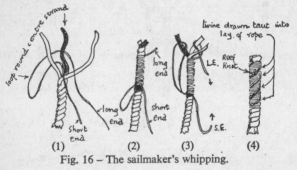

Fig. 16 – The sailmaker's whipping.

Next you draw up the loose loop of twine outside the whipping, and following the lay of the rope, slip it over the end of the same strand that you looped round at the beginning. Haul tight on the *short* end of the twine, and as it comes taut guide it into the lay of the rope.

Now take hold of the short end of twine and bring it up outside the whipping, following the lay of the rope. Tie the two ends of twine together with a reef knot and the whipping is complete. Having described the whipping method, it is only fair to add that one of the features of modern synthetic

rope, nylon, terylene, etc. (see Chapter 15), is that the ends
can be fused solid to prevent unlaying by burning them with
a match. Nevertheless you can't light matches in a gale on
deck, and the conventional method must be learnt.

Finally, the beginner should know how to splice two
pieces of rope together to make one long line. This is done
by means of the short splice. It is the simplest splice, and
is called short to distinguish it from the long splice. In
the latter much more of the rope is unlaid. It is slightly
more difficult, and its advantage over the short splice is that
it does not increase the diameter of the rope, and can, in
consequence, be used for a line that has to run through a
block. However here let us concern ourselves with the
splice that you are most likely to want – the common or
garden short splice.

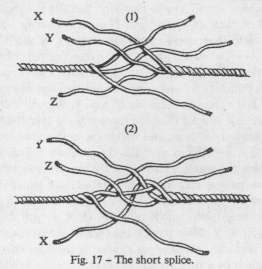

Fig. 17 – The short splice.

Look at the drawings in Figure 17, and try to follow
the method. Take two pieces of rope of equal diameter and
unlay the ends for about six inches. We will call these two

pieces of rope 1 and 2. Place them together so that the three strands of rope 1 are placed between the strands of rope 2, and the three strands of rope 2 are placed between the strands of rope 1. Pull them close together and put a temporary whipping round the standing part of rope 2 and round the strands of rope 1. The first object of the exercise is to place the strands of rope 2 into the standing part of rope 1. We will call these strands X, Y, and Z. Take strand X of rope 2. Pass it over the strand of rope 1 nearest to you and under the next strand of the same rope. Then take strand Y of rope 2 and pass it over the next strand of rope 1 and under the remaining strand in the same way as before. Now do just the same with strand Z of rope 2.

You will find that strand Y lies over the strand under which strand X has been passed, strand Z over the strand under which strand Y was passed in the first instance. This is the first tuck of our splice. Now continue by taking a second tuck. Then take a third tuck, in each case passing each strand over the nearest strand in the standing part of rope 1 and under the next one to it. Three tucks will be enough.

Next, remove the whipping around the standing part of rope 2, and round the strands of rope 1. We will call these strands P, Q, and R. Pass the three strands over the rope 2 strand nearest to them and under the next strand, so that strand Q will be lying over the strand under which strand P has been passed; strand R over the strand under which Q has been passed and under the strand over which P was passed in the first instance.

Take three tucks with strands P, Q, R as you did with strands X, Y, Z. Now cut off the ends of the strands where they project and you have your splice. A short splice reduces the strength of a rope to 85 per cent.

A splice that you must certainly know, as it has hundreds of uses, particularly when fitting out, is the eye splice. This can be made either to form a loop in the end of a rope or to enclose a galvanized iron thimble or go round the shell of a block.

To make the eye splice (see Fig. 18), first whip the rope at about four times its circumference from the end, and having done that unlay the rope down to the whipping. Now, assuming that you are going to make a splice round a thimble, take the latter and form the loop of the rope round its score so that the whipping meets the standing part

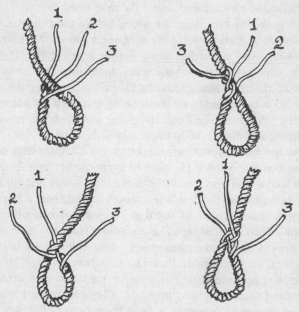

Fig. 18 – The eye splice.

of the rope at the base of the thimble. Now, with a short length of whipping twine, seize the thimble quite lightly to the loop of rope by its crown. Next place the unlaid end of the rope against the standing part so that the unlaid middle strand is on top. Now tuck the middle strand *under* the top strand of the standing part, tucking from right to left. Next pass the left hand strand *over* the top strand and *under* the next strand upon its left. Turn the rope over until the strands already tucked are underneath, and the remaining strand is on the top. Tuck this remaining strand from right to left again *under* that strand in the standing part which has, until now, been left undisturbed. After this first complete tuck has been made, make a second set of tucks, taking each strand from right to left over the nearest strand of the standing part and under the next one.

To make a neat job of the splice, before the third tuck is made each strand should have about a third of its fibres removed, and a further third before making the fourth tuck. This tapers the whole thing down into the standing part of the rope. Care must be taken when taking the last tuck to retain the lay of the rope to enable it to lie more closely. When finished roll the splice underfoot to smooth it down, and finally whip the whole with marline.

As has been mentioned earlier in this Chapter and as is described in Chapter 15, a lot of synthetic cordage is used nowadays, and very good it is. Since it is mostly 3-stranded, the same methods of splicing may be used, but when we come to plaited rope of say 8 or 16 plait this is a different kettle of fish. Plaited ropes have an outer (plaited) layer over a core. It is therefore necessary when splicing to unpick the rope for a sufficient distance to lay bare enough for the type of splice intended. The unlaid threads are then crossed over and tugged tight at intervals. They can be tied with a bit of thread at intervals to hold them better. The last bit should be shaved to form a taper and seized with twine. This method can thus be divided into four simple stages. Let us assume we are making an eye-splice as in Figure 18: (1) divide the yarns and make our 'eye' in the rope; (2) cross the yarns over in a plait; (3) turn the eye over and cross the yarns again; (4) taper and whip. It is simple and makes a good strong splice that increases in strength with the load.

CHAPTER 6

Bending Sails and Hoisting Them

—

WE have discussed what sort of boat you should buy, where to keep her once bought, and we have examined a boat and memorized a lot of names. We have also learnt a few knots. Now let's get down to the business of sailing the vessel you have bought. The first thing to do is to bend on the sails, and this is where our knots will come in handy. Your sails may already be bent to the spars when you buy your boat, but it is more likely that they will be stored away in bags. The first lesson to learn about sails is: treat them with the greatest care. Do not allow them to get dirty; keep them as dry as possible, and do not allow them to get stretched out of shape.

When first I wrote this book there were more gaff-rigged yachts about than there are today. I was, in consequence, when revising for the third edition, tempted to strike out the section in this chapter that deals with bending on a gaff-sail and go straight on to 'Bermudan'. On second thoughts, I see no reason for this. There are still a fair number of gaff-rigged vessels afloat in the world, and in any case, the principle of bending on any sail properly is basically the same. The gaff-rig is a little more complex than the Bermudan. It is quite possible that your first boat may carry a form of gaff-rig, in which case, what follows here will be of value to you. Should you be the proud and impatient owner of a leg o' mutton (Bermudan) sail you can turn to page 73, and start reading from there.

For the present, however, I am assuming that your boat is a small gaff-rigged sloop.

SALLY BROWN

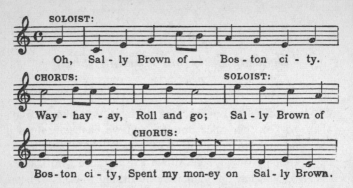

Oh, Sal-ly Brown of — Bos-ton ci-ty.

Way - hay - ay, Roll and go; Sal-ly Brown of

Bos-ton ci-ty, Spent my mon-ey on Sal-ly Brown.

2. *Oh, Sally Brown, you're very pretty,*
   Chorus: *Way-hay-ay, Roll and go;*
   Oh, Sally Brown, you're very pretty,
   Chorus: *Spent my money on Sally Brown.*

3. *Your cheeks are brown, your hair is golden,*
   (Solo repetition and chorus as before).

4. *For Sally Brown she's a bright mulatto,*

5. *Oh, she drinks rum and chews terbakker,*

6. *My Sally Brown's a Creole lady,*

7. *Seven long years I courted Sally,*

8. *Said she, 'My boy, why do you dally?'*

9. *But Sally Brown's a white man's daughter,*

10. *She sent me sailing 'cross the water,*

11. *So Sally Brown, I will not grieve you,*

12. *Oh, Sally Brown, I'll not deceive you.*

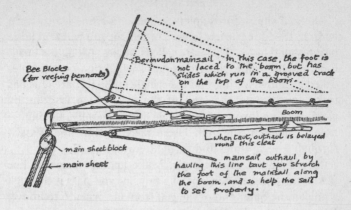

Bee Blocks
(for reefing pennants)

Bermudan mainsail — In this case, the foot is not laced to the boom, but has slides which run in a grooved track on the top of the boom.

Boom

main sheet block

main sheet

when taut, outhaul is belayed round this cleat

mainsail outhaul by hauling this line taut you stretch the foot of the mainsail along the boom, and so help the sail to set properly.

METHOD OF LACING HEAD TO GAFF.

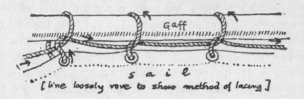

Gaff

s a i l

[line loosely rove to show method of lacing]

METHOD OF
FASTENING HOOP TO
MAINSAIL

BERMUDAN TRACK
ON MAST [with slides.]

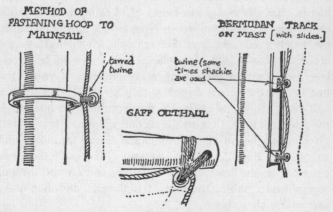

tarred twine

twine (some times shackles are used)

GAFF OUTHAUL

Fig. 19 – Bending on the mainsail.

The gaff rig is sturdy, picturesque, and a fine rig to learn with. In the four corners (clews) of the sail you will find large brass-bound holes. These are called cringles. Along the head, foot, and luff of the sail are a lot of small, brass-bound holes called grommets. First find the cringle at the throat. This has to be fastened to the jaws of the gaff, which is done by passing a line through the cringle and (generally) through a hole or holes in the gaff. Use a piece of thin line. Pass it through several times and tie tightly with a reef knot.

Next find the peak cringle. Make another piece of line fast to the cringle by means of a bowline and pass it through a hole in the outer end of the gaff from underneath to above. Bring the line back to the cringle, pass it through the cringle and pull out the head of the sail. Now tie the end of the line with a clove hitch around both parts of itself between the cringle and the gaff. Do not haul the sail out too tight. Lines shrink in wet weather, and stretching a sail out of shape is fatal as it flattens out the curve that gives it its driving power. Now take a long piece of line – for these purposes you can use hambro line or cod line or any small line made of three-stranded hemp. Hambro line is generally bought in hanks of 15 fathoms. It is fairly expensive. As is described in Chapter 15, synthetic ropes are widely used nowadays. For example, for the purpose we are discussing 3/16th eight-plait Terylene would be excellent. Beginning at the throat, make one end of your long line fast to the throat cringle with a bowline. Then take a half hitch round the gaff at the first grommet. Pass through the first grommet, then to the second grommet, take a half hitch round the gaff, pass through the second grommet, and so on (see Fig. 19). Carry on until you reach the peak cringle. Pass the line through the cringle and around the gaff several times, pulling the peak up to the gaff, and then make fast with a clove hitch.

The head is now bent to the gaff. Next, we must bend

the sail to the mast hoops. For this purpose we use tarred twine called marline. Marline is sold in balls by weight. It is two-stranded and tightly twisted. It has great resistance to the weather. The grommets are seized to the hoops by passing the marline several times through the grommet and round the hoop, and finally passing the marline over itself between the edge of the sail and the hoop, and tying with a reef knot (see Fig. 10).

The sail is bent to the boom in exactly the same manner as to the gaff. First of all the tack is bent to a hole or a ring-bolt in the jaws or the gooseneck, and tied down with a reef knot. Then make fast a light line to the clew cringle with a bowline. This is called the outhaul. It is used to stretch out the foot of the sail. It should be passed over the sheave or pulley at the outer end of the boom and led back and belayed round a cleat on the boom (see Fig. 19).

The foot of the sail should only be pulled out hand tight. Never stretch it out really hard. On a wet day it is better to err on the slack side. Don't try to make the clew of the sail reach the end of the boom. It probably won't, especially if it is a new sail. Spars are built longer than the sails in new boats because sails always get longer as they stretch. It is quite usual for there to be as much as a foot or two of boom sticking out beyond the end of the sail. Now take a length of hambro line; the right length is one and a half times the length of the boom. Make one end fast to the gooseneck or tack cringle with a bowline, and lace it in the same way as the gaff.

Bending a Bermudan mainsail is rather easier than a gaff. For one thing, there being no gaff, all you have to do is to shackle the end of the main halliard on to the head-board of the sail. The luff of the sail has slides bent on to the grommets and these simply run up a track on the after side of the mast (see Fig. 19). Frequently there is a similar track on the boom too. It is generally of light material except for the last foot or two at the outboard end, which is generally made of a heavy material secured to the boom with long, heavy screws. In very small boats and dinghies there is a groove in the back of the mast and in the top of the boom. The luff rope and foot rope of the sail are inserted in these and pulled along so that the sail is held. It is a simple and effective method.

The outhaul (see Fig. 19) generally terminates in an eye splice which is attached to the clew cringle by means of a shackle. Bear in mind that the outhaul serves the purpose of pulling the foot of the sail out, and another device should be used to hold the clew of the sail down to the boom. Do not use one line for both these purposes. If the sail reaches out far enough along the boom for the slides at the end grommets (sometimes there is a special carriage bent on the last grommet) to be in the heavy track, no other holding down device is necessary. But should the foot of the sail be short, the clew cringle must be secured to the boom with cod line as described in bending a gaff mainsail. In the leech of the sail you will find a light line, running from the head of the sail to a point just above the clew. It is called the leech line. It is sewn into a pocket in the leech and leaves this pocket through a grommet just above the clew of the sail. Its function is to tauten up and pucker the leech if it is too loose. This rarely occurs. Most leeches are on the tight side, and it is better to leave well alone. Never use it for reefing.

The next thing to do is put the battens in the pockets. These are pockets sewn into the leech of the sail extending forward at right angles to it. In these are placed thin strips of wood of varying lengths called battens. The longest battens go in the middle of the leech. The battens should be an inch or two shorter than the batten pockets, as if they touch the end of the pocket they tend to make a hard line in the sail when it is set.

Jibs are bent on simply by snapping the hooks on the

luff on to the forestay, beginning with the tack and working upwards to the head of the sail. The halliard will have a snap hook or an eye splice with a shackle by means of which it is bent on to the head of the sail. The tack is generally snapped or secured by a shackle to a ring in the deck at the bottom of the forestay.

The jib sheets are snapped or shackled on to the clew cringle and led back through blocks or fairleads on the side decks to cleats on the deck alongside the cockpit coaming, or sometimes on the side of the coaming itself. Sometimes, especially in larger boats where the jib takes a bit more handling, the jib sheets are doubled. Two wire pennants with a block spliced into one end of each, and an eye splice at the other, are both shackled through the eye splices to the clew cringle. The sheets then lead from a point on the side deck on either side of the boat up through the blocks and so back through the fairleads to the cleats on the cockpit coaming. This gives added power when sheeting in (see Fig. 7).

Another means of obtaining additional power is by the use of metal sheet winches situated on either side of the cockpit. You simply take a turn round the winch before heaving. They work on the ratchet principle, so you must make certain you take a turn in the right direction – usually clockwise (see Fig. 7). Sometimes, generally in racing boats, there is a pennant on the tack of the jib which reeves through a block at the foot of the forestay back aft, where its after end is spliced to a block. Through this block is rove a line made fast on the forecastle. This line comes back from the block to a cleat on deck. It is called the jib tack downhaul; in large craft, a purchase is used. The jib halliard, which is generally belayed round a cleat on the mast, or on deck at the foot of the mast, is sometimes terminated in an eye splice which loops over a hook in the deck. This is often the case where you have a tack downhaul. The object of the tack downhaul is to tauten up the luff of the sail. It is neces-

sary to have the leading edge of luff of the sail straight when
going to windward, and not a series of curves or arches as it
would be if the luff were slack. It also looks much better.
Where there is no tack downhaul the luff is pulled straight by
hauling taut on the jib halliard, which is sometimes fitted
with a small purchase to give additional power. This latter
is in fact the most usual method in small boats. The jib
sheets and tack downhaul are illustrated in Fig. 7. Sometimes a head downhaul is rove too. Its purpose is to haul
the jib down on deck quickly. It is simply a line rove up
through a block at the foot of the forestay, up (running
parallel to the forestay) through each spring hook to the head
of the sail where it is bent on. It is not really necessary in small
boats and it increases the amount of gear on the fo'c'sle.

In Chapter 8 we shall discuss which sail to hoist first.
For the present, we will assume that conditions are such that
the mainsail is to be hoisted first. To hoist a gaff-rigged
mainsail you start by casting the main sheet off its cleat.
Then haul on the topping lift until the boom swings clear of
the boom crutches. The boom crutches provide a support
for the boom when the mainsail is lowered (see Fig. 3).

Belay the topping lift, unship the boom crutch and stow
it away. There should be a proper place for it, just as there
should be for everything on board. 'A place for everything
and everything in its place.'

Now it is usual for the peak halliard to lead down the
starboard side of the mast and the throat halliard down the
port. Memorize the saying 'There is no red port left, it
has all gone down my throat'.* That reminds us that the
left side of a vessel (when looking ahead) is the Port side;
that the Port navigation light is red (the Starboard is green)
and that the throat halliard leads down the Port hand side
of the mast.

* Teetotallers should read: 'There is some red port left, but it *ain't*
going down *my* throat!'

Now take hold of these two halliards. Pull evenly on both, keeping the gaff horizontal. If your boat is equipped with two topping lifts, the gaff must go up between them. If the sail sticks on the way up, it is probably because one of the mast hoops is sticking on the mast. The cure for this is a thin coating of hard grease on the inner rim of the forward side of each mast hoop. A temporary remedy is to let the throat drop suddenly for about a foot. This will generally free it.

Continue hoisting until the luff of the sail is stretched fairly tight. Belay the throat halliard and hoist the peak until deep wrinkles appear in the throat of the sail. The general direction of these wrinkles should be more or less parallel to the luff. If the wrinkles are parallel to the leech the peak is too low. Unless wrinkles appear and run parallel to the luff, the peak is not hoisted high enough.

Having hoisted the peak sufficiently, belay the halliard. There should be cleats on or near the mast for all these lines. You should now slack off the topping lift or it will cut into the belly of the sail.

If your boat has a Bermudan mainsail, you hoist with one halliard only, hoisting until the luff is stretched taut. The wrinkles in the Bermudan sail should run parallel to the luff as well. You must not hoist so high that these wrinkles disappear. If they do, the luff is too tight and must be eased off a little. The slides on the luff of the Bermudan mainsail are apt sometimes to stick in the track – generally at the joints or where a screw has pulled loose and is sticking up into the track. The temporary remedy is to work the sail up and down gently, and ease it over the tricky spot on the track. When you return to harbour, go up the mast in a Bo's'un's chair (a short plank slung horizontally from a line), examine the track, and see that the defect is put right.

If the wind is at all strong, you should take great care

to look aloft when hoisting. When partly hoisted, Bermudan mainsails have a habit of flapping about and fouling the runners and spreaders on the mast. So hoist slowly and carefully, and if the sail catches round anything, lower it again until it is freed. If you continue to hoist in the hope that it will free itself, you will probably tear the sail.

The jib is hoisted in the same manner as a Bermudan mainsail. If your boat has a purchase on the jib halliard or a jib tack downhaul to enable you to get a beautifully straight luff, do not haul so tight as to remove all the wrinkles that run parallel to the luff. You will be able to get it straight without doing this.

Sails are cut with a roach. Examine yours now and see they are properly roached. That is to say that the curve of the leech should be convex, and should extend out beyond a straight line from the head to the clew, or, in the case of a gaff sail, from the peak to the clew. The foot is also roached.

Having hoisted your sails you must coil down the halliards. In most boats the coils are hung up on the cleats or tucked under the standing part of the halliard. Before lowering sail always place them on deck, with the end leading to the cleat at the top of the coil. This is called capsizing a coil. The halliard can then run easily up the mast as the sail comes down.

Having learnt how to bend and hoist sail, we must pause for a moment and consider in the next chapter why a boat sails at all; the answer is not so obvious as it might first appear!

CAN'T YOU DANCE THE POLKA

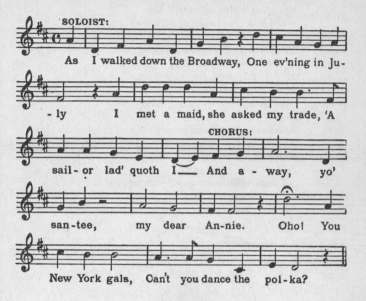

SOLOIST: As I walked down the Broadway, One ev'ning in Ju-ly I met a maid, she asked my trade, 'A sail-or lad' quoth I— CHORUS: And a-way, yo' san-tee, my dear An-nie. Oho! You New York gals, Can't you dance the pol-ka?

2.   *To Nelligan's I took her,*
I did not spare expense;
I bought her a slap-up supper
That cost me ninety cents.
      Chorus: *And away yo' santee,* etc.

3.   *Said she, ' You lime-juice sailor,*
Now see me home you may.'
But when at last we reached her door,
Then to me she did say
      Chorus: *And away, yo' santee,* etc.

4. *'My flash man he's a Yankee,*
   With his hair clipped down behind;
   He wears a brass-bound jacket,
   And sails in the Blackball Line.'
       Chorus: *And away, yo' santee,* etc.

5. *'He's homeward bound this evening,*
   And with me he will stay,
   So kiss me, dear, for much I fear,
   You'll have to sail away.'
       Chorus: *And away, yo' santee,* etc.

6. *I kissed her hard and proper*
   Before her flash man came,
   And said, 'Farewell, you naughty gel,
   I know your little game.'
       Chorus: *And away, yo' santee,* etc.

CHAPTER 7

The Theory of Sailing

—

THE earliest craft that sailed had a square sail and sailed dead before the wind (see Fig. 20). The Nile boats used to sail upstream *against* the current and lower the sail to return *with* the current.

The Vikings, in their long fierce ships, had square sails too, although there is evidence that they knew how to sail on other points as well as before the wind.

But the fact remains that the fore-and-aft rig is a comparatively modern invention. Indeed, long after it was developed, vessels that habitually made trans-ocean voyages retained the square rig. A square-rigged ship behaves better than a fore-and-after when the wind is abaft the beam, and these voyages were generally in the path of the prevailing winds (Trades; Westerlies), which could be relied on to blow from the same quarter fairly continuously.

The first people to develop the fore-and-aft rig were the Arabs. The 'baggara' or Arab dhow is probably the father of the fore-and-aft rig. It is certainly the father of lateen-rigged vessels. Lateen-rigged boats carry short masts and their sails are hoisted on enormous yards that rake high in the air abaft the masts. All lateen sails can be sheeted into an almost fore-and-aft position, and the Arabs' boats were quite efficient on the wind as well as before it.

But the true fore-and-aft rig came into being a long time later. (By the true fore-and-aft rig I mean a sail whose forward edge is secured to a mast or stay on which it pivots.) Seamen are renowned for their conservatism, and hundreds of years passed before the fore-and-aft rig came into general

use. Then, slowly, ships changed their form. Keels were
built to give lateral resistance to the water and prevent the
ship moving sideways when the wind was on the beam.
The high poops and forecastles were lowered so as to offer
less wind resistance, and at last the rather amazing fact
was discovered that a boat may be sailed against the force
that drives it – the wind. The reason why a boat can sail
against the wind was not fully understood until the advent
of the aeroplane. When it was known that it is not the wind's
pressure *underneath* the wings of an aeroplane that lifts it

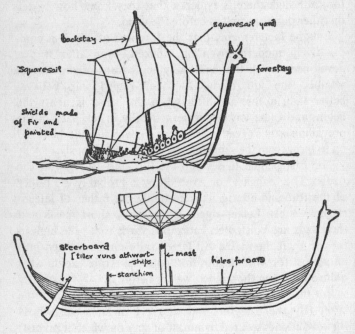

Fig. 20 – The early craft: a Viking ship (not to scale).
The Viking ships were clinker-built; the Gokstad ship (which is pre-
served today) was about 75 feet in length and had a beam of 16 feet.

into the air, but the vacuum on the *upper* surface of the wings caused by the air flowing over the curved surface, it was soon realized that the same argument applies to the sails of boats. The wind blowing past the leeward side of a sail gives a lift against the direction of the wind – a forward lift in fact. But when sailing to windward only a small amount of the actual force of the wind is utilized in driving the ship. Much of this force runs to waste along the sails'

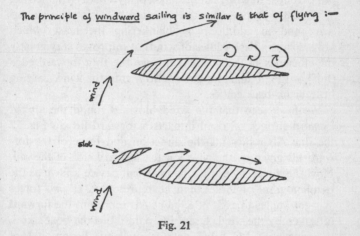

The principle of <u>windward</u> sailing is similar to that of flying :—

wind

slot

wind

Fig. 21

surface; some being wasted in trying to push the hull sideways, and some in heeling the ship over against the downward pull of her ballast.

The principal function of the jib when sailing close-hauled is to guide the wind round the leeward side of the mainsail. If the wind were not so guided it would not flow evenly round the mainsail and eddies or 'turbulence' would form on the leeward side. It is interesting to note that the slots on the wing of certain types of aircraft perform much the same function as the jib of a yacht. They guide the airflow round the wing of the aircraft. If the air were not so guided when the wing is at a large angle of incidence, there would be turbulence starting at the after end of the wing in the same way as with a sail. The result would be that the suction on the upper surface of the wing would be diminished until the 'lift' would disappear and the aircraft would stall (see Fig. 21). Turbulence on the leeward after side of a sail is indicated by the flapping of the sail. It may be caused by a badly-setting sail – one that has perhaps stretched out of shape, or by a badly trimmed jib.

Thus the jib performs the function of a slot in a slotted wing and in addition, by blanketing the mast (which always causes back eddies of wind), it improves very greatly the efficiency of the sail plane, since the thin forward edge (luff) of the jib makes a good 'entry' into the wind, causing little or no back eddies.

We have seen that the wind blowing round the arched leeward surface of a sail imparts a forward lift. In Fig. 22 the line AB represents the direction and force of the forward lift given by the wind on the leeward side of the sail. Now this force, by using a geometrical device known as the parallelogram of forces, can be represented as two forces at right angles to each other. Let AB represent the forward lift given by the wind. Draw BC parallel to the boat's keel, the length of BC being proportional to the amount of forward drive in AB. Draw AC at right angles to the boat's keel. AC is proportional to the amount of leeward drive in AB. Draw AD equal to and parallel to BC and join DB. Now the hull of the boat is so shaped that it offers very little resistance to that part of the wind's force represented by AD and a great deal of resistance to that part represented by AC. The result is that the boat will move along AD, except in so far as its lateral resistance is overcome by the force AC. This failure of lateral resistance is called leeway. All boats make a certain amount of leeway when close-hauled. The amount varies according to the plan and area of the sails and the form of the hull, and of course is much affected by weather conditions, the state of the sea, etc. With regard to hull form, depth is of more consequence than length in this connexion. If you were to increase the area of a dinghy's centreboard without increasing its depth, you would not improve her windward performance to any great extent.

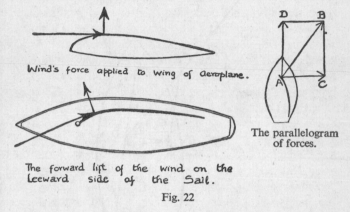

Wind's force applied to wing of aeroplane.

The forward lift of the wind on the leeward side of the Sail.

The parallelogram of forces.

Fig. 22

But to return to our problem. We have seen how the forward lift given by the wind acting on the leeward side of the sail can be translated by means of a parallelogram of forces into forward thrust and leeway.

The yacht's principal driving force is obtained in this way, but she also gets a certain amount of forward drive from the wind acting on the weather side of the sail. Once again we must resort to our old friend the parallelogram of forces. Fig. 23 shows a vessel close-hauled on the port tack. AB is the sail and CD the wind. (We will assume that the wind or part of it strikes the sail at D).

Let CD be the force of the wind and AB the plane of the sail. From A draw AF at right angles to the plane of the sail (AB) to cut CD at F. From F draw a line parallel to AD, and with centre F and radius AD cut this line at E. Join ED, which will be parallel to FA. Here, then, is our parallelogram of forces, ADEF. The wind force CD has been resolved into two forces at right angles to each other, AD and DE. Now AD represents the force that is running to waste along the surface of the sail. This does not concern us. What does

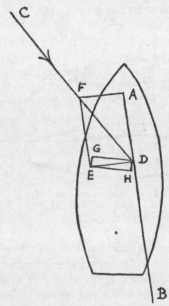

Fig. 23 – Parallelogram of forces, showing forward drive obtained from wind acting on windward side of sail.

concern us is DE, a force acting at right angles to the sail. Take ED and resolve it once more into another pair of forces at right angles to each other, GD and HD. GD is of no interest to us, as it merely tries to drive the hull sideways, but HD is our actual forward-driving force. Notice how small it is compared with the amount of force that is wasted in various directions. This diagram shows why a ship heels over so much when going to windward. The force

GD is employed in heeling the yacht and trying to cause leeway. The hull, however, is shaped so that it offers the least forward resistance possible, and the greatest possible resistance sideways, so that the small forward force HD is able to push the boat easily through the water, while the larger force GD produces nothing worse than a little leeway.

In this explanation I have left out the apparent wind and dealt only with the true wind. By apparent wind I mean the direction from which the wind appears to come once the ship has started to move ahead. As the ship moves ahead faster, the wind will appear to draw more and more ahead, and it will be under the influence of this 'apparent wind' that any forward movement will continue. The apparent wind will continue to draw ahead until the water resistance set up by the hull form of the yacht to any forward movement exactly balances the forward-acting force. When this point is reached the only way in which an increase of speed can be obtained is by increasing the amount of sail carried (assuming that the wind remains constant) and so pushing back the point of balance between the drive of the wind and the resistance of the water.

Only about 25 per cent of the actual force of the wind is utilized in driving the ship forward, and a very small proportion of that is actual forward-driving force. Careful experiments in wind tunnels have shown that 75 per cent of the force driving a yacht is derived from the suction or negative pressure on the leeward side of the sails. The combination of these two is what gets the boat to windward. No boat will sail directly against the wind, the nearness with which it will sail being determined by a number of factors of hull and sail design. Most vessels will sail about four points off the wind or roughly 45 degrees to the wind's direction. It will be seen therefore that to sail a course against the wind, you must sail 45 degrees from it, first in one direction and then in the other – a sort of zig-zagging progress. This is called tacking. All racing vessels are what is called close-winded. It is also known from wind tunnel experiments that the leading edge (luff) of the sail is the most important by far where windward sailing is concerned. Consequently the modern trend in racing craft is to shorten the boom, keeping the high mast. The way a sail sets plays a big part in a boat's efficiency on the wind. A beautifully roached sail will take on a good aerodynamic curve (like the wing of an aeroplane) and the boat will point close and sail fast.

The three points of sailing – before the wind, with the wind on the beam, and against the wind – are known respectively as running, reaching, and close-hauled. So much for theory; now let's get down to the business of actually sailing the boat.

ODDS AND ENDS OF SALTY WISDOM CULLED FROM MANY SOURCES

When buying, assume a ship is rotten until you have satisfied yourself that she is sound.

Do not have a bright compass light. Use a luminous card, or better still, arrange a method of screening the light.

A celluloid (transparent) chart-holder is a valuable asset. It can be written on with a grease pencil or by roughening the surface and using an ordinary pencil.

When racing, don't try to sail as close to the wind as the other man; concentrate on keeping you own ship sailing as fast as possible.

Have plenty of handrails both in the cabin and on deck.

Don't judge a boat by paint and varnish.

You will generally sight lights at 2 miles or so less than the visibility distances given on the chart, as these are made out from a height of 15 feet.

Take as much care of your sail bags as your sails.

Don't wait for a dusting before you bother to track down and cure leaks in the fore hatch, skylight, etc.

It is worth almost any sacrifice to carry your dinghy on deck.

Whether racing or cruising, a good watch is essential.

Avoid gadget-mongers – your own gadgets will be more than enough.

Don't arrive with three suitcases when on a cruising week-end by invitation. Keep your gear as small as possible.

Always carry oilies. Short oilies are easier to work in than long. In very wet weather you can use oily trousers with them.

Don't wear white flannels and a peaked cap when sailing a 14-foot dinghy.

Don't wear white flannels and a peaked cap when sailing an ocean racer.

Don't wear white flannels and a peaked cap.

Always carry a first-aid kit and include a bottle of rum with it.

Don't try and get Customs officers drunk; they are used to it, and in any case will treat you perfectly fairly.

Develop a system of counting seconds for timing lights reasonably accurately without a stop watch. For example 'one-and-two-and-three' – or any other system will do.

Never think that any one form of sailing is superior to another, unless it's your own.

Do not form conclusions from the courses of other ships at sea. Remember the man who followed a barge and found she had gone to load sand.

Because you see a buoy when and where expected, don't assume that it is the right one.

Marine worms love centreboard cases, and rudder trunks.

A bright yellow sky at sunset foretells wind. A pale yellow sky foretells rain.

A pale green complexion at any time at sea foretells a steadily growing lack of interest in matters navigational.

CHAPTER 8

Getting Under Way

—

LET us consider first how we are going to leave our moorings. This calls for cool judgement, particularly if the anchorage is a crowded one. It does not matter whether the yacht is riding to her own anchor or to the riding scope of a mooring – the problems are the same. There is a rule of thumb for leaving moorings. It concerns the direction of the wind in relation to the tide: when the wind and the tide are in the same direction, set the mainsail before dropping moorings. When wind and tide are in opposition, get away under jib and hoist mainsail later.

The explanation is simple. If wind and tide are in the same direction, the yacht will be behaving like a weathervane. The mainsail will be easily hoisted and, once hoisted, it will flap gently in the breeze. If wind and tide are in opposition and the current is sufficiently strong to cause the boat to be more or less stern to wind it will not only be difficult to hoist the mainsail, which will blow all round the shrouds as soon as the wind fills it, but the ship will immediately start to sail. In this instance drop the moorings, hoist the jib and sail away under it until you have room to turn head to wind and hoist your mainsail in comfort.

Unless you have a racing type of yacht, you will not be able to beat to windward well under jib alone, and you will have to sail down wind to find room to turn. A racing boat can generally go to windward in normal conditions under headsails alone. Before getting under way, have a careful look round the anchorage. Note the positions of the other vessels and make certain what the tide is doing. Having

made up your mind on a plan of action, put it into practice
unhesitatingly.

Now let us consider some situations you will probably
meet with when getting under way:

Situation A. (Fig. 24.)

It is slack water, therefore no tide, and there is plenty
of room to manoeuvre (called 'sea-room'). Your yacht,
a Bermudan sloop of about 4 tons, is riding head to wind.
You set mainsail and have the jib ready for instant hoisting.

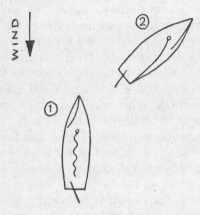

Fig. 24 – Situation A.

As soon as the main is set, the yacht may start to sheer
gently about with the sail filling first on one side and then
on the other. Let us assume you wish to get away to starboard, that is, on the port tack, with the wind blowing on
the port side of the sails. Hoist the jib, but don't drop
your moorings. Have the port jib sheet hauled in (Fig. 24
(1)). If she is sheering about wait until she has just finished
a starboard 'tack'. Put the tiller over to port (Hard-a-
starboard), then the wind, blowing on the port side of the
jib, will push the bow away to starboard. Now let go your
moorings. When the mainsail is full and she is well away,

slack the port jib sheet and haul in the starboard one. Then steady your helm and trim the main sheet. (Fig. 24 (2)). If the yacht is not sheering about, you can haul her ahead on the buoy rope (with the helm hard-a-starboard) and as the bow pays off to starboard, let go the moorings.

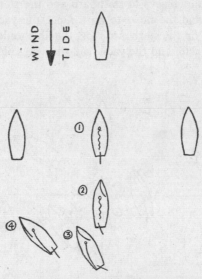

Fig. 25 – Situation B.

Situation B. (Fig. 25).
Let us now consider a more complicated situation. Your yacht is riding to wind and tide, and has other craft moored close to her on either hand. They are close enough to make it very risky trying to 'cast', as it is called, for one tack or another across their bows. The tide will almost certainly carry you on to them. Here, then, the best thing to do is to hoist the mainsail, and have the jib ready for hoisting. Then let go your mooring and drop quietly astern on the tide. Then, when there is sufficient room to cast, hoist the jib and sheet it in. If you intend to cast to

port, sheet the jib in to starboard. As soon as the wind takes
effect the yacht will begin to move astern faster than the
tide. This is called a 'sternboard'. Now, remembering that
when going astern the rudder will have the opposite effect
to when the yacht is going ahead, move the tiller to port.
Thus the rudder goes to starboard and the stern swings to
starboard, and the bows to port. Once the yacht has paid
off like this on the starboard tack, the jib should be sheeted
in the port side, and the yacht can then be sailed clear (see
Fig. 25 (4)).

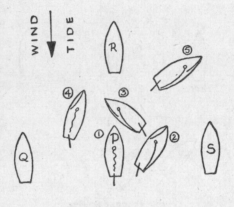

Fig. 26 – Situation C.

Situation C. (Fig. 26).
Here is another situation that may easily arise. Your ship
is at P. Q, R, S, and T are other yachts at moorings. Let
us suppose that you want to get away to starboard on the

port tack. S is so close that once again it is probable that the tide would carry you on to her bows – you would not be able to 'weather' her, as the correct expression says. Q is just as much in the way as S, while T prevents you from dropping astern.

Here, the best plan is to make a tack or two, so as to gain a bit of ground to windward, while still actually on your moorings. Hoist the mainsail and jib and sheet the jib to port. Helm hard-a-starboard. The yacht immediately sheers away towards S until she is brought up by the mooring chain tightening. This will pull her bow round (Fig. 26 (2) and (3)). Slack away the port jib sheet and put the helm hard-a-port to help her round. She is now on the starboard tack and sailing towards a point somewhere ahead of Q. When the chain tightens again it will pull her round (4) and then if, as you should be, you are in a position from which you can weather S on the port tack, you can let go your moorings. By doing this your boat will be both farther up to windward and farther from S, and consequently should be able to weather S without difficulty (5). If you find that you are only just going to clear S, remember that once the yacht's midships has passed S, you can swing the stern clear by putting the tiller to port.

Situation D. (Fig. 27).
There is another way in which we can make use of a sternboard to get us clear from a crowded anchorage. We are at A, and B, C, D, and E are four other yachts all moored close to us. In this instance we want to pass astern of D.

Hoist mainsail and jib, check the sheering of the yacht with the tiller, and, when she is lying quietly head to wind, let go moorings. She will slowly drift astern. Keep her course straight by using the tiller and jib sheets as necessary, and once again, don't forget that the rudder has the opposite effect when going astern to that when going ahead.

When she is in a suitable position to pass clear of D's stern, helm hard-a-starboard and haul in the port jib sheet (2). This will pay the bows off to starboard and her stern will move to port. Now steady the helm, sheet in the jib to starboard and trim the main sheet (3). The yacht will pass easily under D's stern (4).

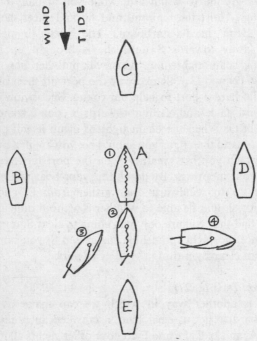

Fig. 27 – Situation D.

This last manoeuvre should not be attempted until you have got to know your ship. Also it is unwise to attempt manoeuvres of this sort in anything of a breeze. A sudden squall will cause a boat that has little or no way on her to heel over to an alarming extent. If it is blowing, keep way on the ship. Way means stability.

So far we have dealt with one or two typical situations when wind and tide are in the same direction. Now let us consider what to do when they are in opposition.

Situation E. (Fig. 28).

Your yacht is at A and you wish to get away from your mooring. There are no other craft in the immediate vicinity. The yacht is tide ridden against the wind.

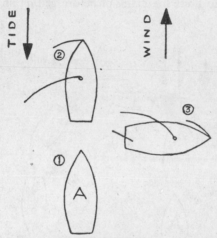

Fig. 27 – Situation E – wrong way.

Now supposing we carried on as we have been accustomed, and hoisted the mainsail – what would happen? The sail would wrap itself round the shroud and, if a gaff sail, the gaff would swing broad off. As soon as the wind filled the sail, the boat would begin to drive ahead, until when sufficient sail was hoisted she would sail out to the limit of the riding scope of her moorings, swing broadside on, sheer away and be carried up wind by the tide to repeat the vicious circles (2) and (3).

There is only one safe way (see Fig. 29). Prepare the mainsail for a quick hoist. Drop the moorings, hoist the jib, and sail away to leeward until there is sufficient sea-room for you to luff up (bring the bows up into the wind) and hoist the mainsail (1), (2), (3), (4), and (5).

Supposing however that the yacht is tide ridden and the wind is across the tide. If the wind is abaft the beam, let go moorings, hoist jib and luff up at once and set the mainsail. If the wind is on the beam or just before it, it is usually possible to hoist the mainsail before getting under way by

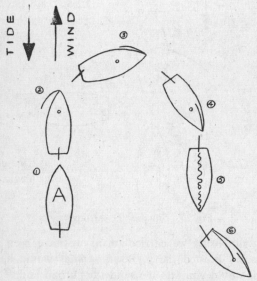

Fig. 29 – Situation E – right way.

spilling the wind out of it. This can be done in a gaff-rigged ship by lowering the peak and topping up the boom. In a Bermudan craft the lee runner should be slacked right off and the boom swung broad off so that the sail presents very little of its surface to the wind. In a ship with a loose-footed mainsail the tack can be triced up with a tricing line as high as may be necessary to keep the sail from having any effect on the ship. With the mainsail hoisted you can hoist the jib, let go moorings, port the helm, trim mainsail and jib, and away.

In all cases the important thing is to prevent the mainsail from having any effect until the mooring has been slipped or the anchor broken out of ground.

In all these cases where I have referred to slipping or letting go moorings, the procedure is the same if the yacht is at anchor, except of course that it is not quite so simple. The anchor has to be hove in either by a winch or by hand. There are several excellent winches on the market, and if your yacht is of 5 tons or more it is well worth fitting one of these winches. Heaving in 20 fathoms of cable with a three-knot tide running can be an exhausting and slow business! For small yachts up to 5 tons Worth's chain pawl, which can be fitted either on deck or on the fairlead at the stem head, is the best. For larger yachts a geared winch is better. It should be borne in mind that the anchor should be hove short first. Take a sounding with the lead line (see Fig. 37). If the depth is 2 fathoms heave in on the anchor until you have just about $2\frac{1}{2}$ fathoms of cable out; then, when the time comes to weigh anchor, it can be done quickly. If there is a strong tide running and there is not a good winch aboard, sail the yacht on alternate tacks up to the anchor, getting in a bit of cable each time, and taking a turn round the samson post in the fo'c'sle as she goes about. If the anchor will not break out of the ground easily, the above method of 'tacking up to it' will usually 'sail it out' quite happily.

Finally – there is the question of getting under way from a jetty or wharf. If you are lying head to wind the position is simplified. Set mainsail and jib, haul the yacht along the quay for a few feet to get steerage way, use the helm to cant the bow away from the jetty, bear off with a boat hook, and as soon as the sails are full, let go the last rope and sail away.

If there is a following wind, the mainsail should not be set and the yacht must be manoeuvred clear of the wharf under jib alone, using a boat hook to bear away.

These two situations present no difficulties. It is a bit harder when the wind is setting on to the jetty. In this instance run the kedge anchor out in the dinghy to a point as far away as possible and at right angles to the jetty face. When the anchor has been laid, cast off mooring ropes from the quay and haul out to the kedge anchor. The yacht will then be lying to an anchor and you can proceed in the usual way, bearing in mind the fact that the jetty is still comparatively close!

The functions of mooring ropes will be dealt with in Chapter 12, but very briefly the last ropes to let go should be those which are necessary only to hold the yacht in a position from which she can best be got under way. It is generally simplest, unless there is someone standing on the quay who will let go your line for you, to have the last lines made fast inboard, taken ashore round a bollard, or through a ring-bolt, and so back to the yacht, from where they can be let go quickly and easily.

LEAVE HER, JOHNNY

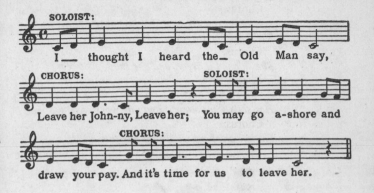

SOLOIST:
I __ thought I heard the __ Old Man say,

CHORUS: Leave her John-ny, Leave her; SOLOIST: You may go a-shore and

CHORUS: draw your pay. And it's time for us to leave her.

2. You can make her fast and pack your gear,
       Chorus: *Leave her, Johnny, leave her,*
    You can have her moored 'longside the pier,
       Chorus: *And it's time for us to leave her.*

3. The winds were foul, the trip was long,
       Chorus.
    And before we leave we'll sing a song,
       Chorus.

4. We'll sing, oh, may we never be,
       Chorus.
    On a hungry ship the likes of she,
       Chorus.

5. The food was bad, the wages low,
       Chorus.
    And now ashore again we'll go.
       Chorus.

6.   *The bunks were hard and the watches long,*
        Chorus.
    The seas were high and the winds were strong,
        Chorus.

7.   *She'd neither stay, nor steer nor wear,*
        Chorus.
    She shipped it green and she made us swear,
        Chorus.

8.   *Her sails were stowed and our work is done,*
        Chorus.
    So now on shore we'll find our fun,
        Chorus.

CHAPTER 9

Before the Wind

—

THE first ships sailed before the wind; the wind, blowing into their sails from behind, drove the ship along in front of it. As it is in many respects the easiest point of sailing, we will start with it.

The first thing you must do is to determine the direction of the wind itself. This can be done by watching the burgee or small flag at the mast-head. Another method is by tying a piece of ribbon as high up as you can on one of the shrouds or the weather runner (see Fig. 30). After you have gained a bit of experience, you will develop wind-direction consciousness. You will sense the wind on one cheek more than another, you may feel it at the back of your neck, even on your hands.

Another clue as to the wind's direction can be found by watching the waves. Waves come almost directly from the direction of the wind. They do not roll exactly down wind, however. There is always a slight variation between the wind's direction and that of the waves. And once again practice makes perfect. The experienced sailor can judge the wind's direction from watching the waves.

To sail your ship before the wind, pay out the main sheet until the mainsail is roughly at right angles to the fore-and-aft line of the boat. Note that the mainsail should be at right angles; not the main boom. The top half of the sail invariably sags forward. If you paid out the main sheet until the boom were at right angles to the boat, the top half of the sail would be sagging ahead and you would be losing driving power. If you are sailing dead before the wind the

Helmsman steers carefully to avoid getting wind on lee side of sail and so gybing. He feels wind on back of neck, watches Burgee, piece of ribbon on shroud

Jib blanketed by Mainsail

It is difficult to estimate real strength of wind when running

Keep wind on opposite quarter to Boom.

Dangers when Running: Excessive rolling and being 'pooped' by wave breaking into Cockpit.

Fig. 30 – Running.

mainsail may be paid out either to port or starboard, but preferably the wind should be on one quarter or the other, the mainsail being out on the opposite side.

The jib sheet should be trimmed so that the jib will be nearly at right angles to the fore-and-aft line of the boat. However, you will probably find that, when running before the wind, the jib will be completely blanketed by the mainsail and will just flap idly. After you have gained some experience and have become fairly adept at running, you can spread the jib out on the opposite side of the vessel to the mainsail, by using a whisker pole, or in some cases a boat hook. A whisker pole is a light spar with jaws on one end like a gaff and a spike on the other. The spike is pushed through the clew of the jib, and the jaws rest against the mast (see Fig. 31). The whisker pole holds the jib out at more or less right angles to the boat. The jib is most effective used this way. A boat hook is used in the same way except that this necessitates lashing the inboard end to the mast. To make the boat hook or whisker pole stay in place, it is necessary to trim the jib sheet to put a strain up the spar, and thus hold it against the mast.

If your vessel has runners, you must slack off the lee runner, to prevent it cutting into the belly of the sail. When running, the full weight of the sail is forward and the wind tends to drive the bow downwards. Always move your passengers and crew further aft to counter-balance this.

In the case of centreboard craft, the centreboard should be raised. Most boats will sail at their fastest (when running) with the centreboard raised entirely, but if she shows a tendency to yaw or swing off her course in either direction, it is wise to lower the board a quarter of its full depth. It is also important to see that the weather runner and, if there is one, the standing backstay, are set up taut, for these take the extra strain on the mast.

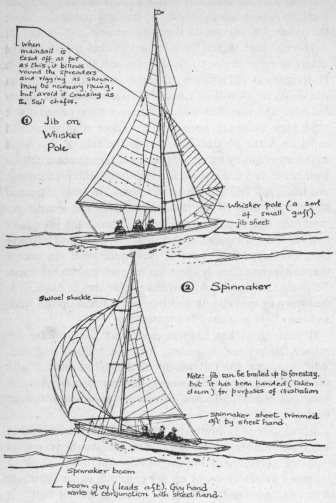

When mainsail is eased off as far as this, it billows round the spreaders and rigging as shown. May be necessary racing, but avoid it cruising as the sail chafes.

① Jib on Whisker Pole

Whisker pole (a sort of small gaff).

jib sheet

② Spinnaker

Swivel shackle

Note: jib can be brailed up to forestay, but it has been handed (taken down) for purposes of illustration

spinnaker sheet trimmed aft by sheet hand.

Spinnaker boom

boom guy (leads aft). Guy hand works in conjunction with sheet hand.

Fig. 31 – Making the most of a following wind.

So long as the wind is not quite aft, but is 10 degrees or more on the weather quarter, everything is quite simple: the yacht runs along and can be kept on her course with ease. But if the wind is at all fluky in direction or if there is any sea running that may roll the yacht off her course so that the wind is blowing from the same side as that on which the mainsail is out, beware! This is called sailing 'by the lee'. You must watch carefully that the wind does not catch the mainsail on its foreside and swing the whole sail violently across with great force on to the other tack. This is called gybing, and in strong winds is dangerous. With the violence of such a swing the boom drives across with great force, taking up hard against the runner and backstay, and may part them or snap off the boom itself, or even endanger the whole mast.

However, there is no need for this gruesome catalogue of accidents to take place. Careful watching of the wind's direction when running is the answer. Keep it just over the quarter on the opposite side to the mainsail.

On the other hand, an intentional gybe is quite simple and safe if done in the following way.

Call out 'Gybe-oh!' to warn all on board to watch out for the boom swinging over, and put the helm 'up' (into the wind),* and haul in on the main sheet. Set up the late lee runner, which is now the weather, and ease off the new lee runner. As the yacht turns, haul in the main sheet hard until the wind has passed the stern of the yacht and she is sailing 'by the lee'. Belay the main sheet quickly, and as the wind comes over definitely on to the new quarter, the boom

---

* Note: If the yacht is sailing on the port tack, to turn up into the wind you would put the tiller to starboard. Now the starboard side will be lower than the port owing to the heeling over to starboard of the ship, therefore this is called putting the helm 'down'. Vice versa, putting the helm over the high or windward side of the ship (in this case to port) is called putting the helm 'up'.

will swing over. As there will be very little of the main sheet out, however, it will not do any damage. Now you can pay out the main sheet and trim mainsail and jib as necessary for the new course. If the jib was winged out with a whisker pole, the latter should be unshipped before gybing.

There are two other dangers to be guarded against when running before the wind; broaching to and rolling. In the case of broaching to, you will find that this is most likely to occur in a seaway. You will be sailing along quite happily when suddenly the boat starts to come around into the wind with the boom broad off. The ship being heeled over, the boom dips into the water and may start to pull the boat over. This is dangerous, since as soon as the boom is in the water, the rudder becomes useless. The only safeguard is alertness. As in the case of gybing, watch your steering, and at the first tendency for the boat to broach to, check her with the rudder. As with gybing, there is no need to worry if you watch your steering. It is easier than it sounds, and the dangers of gybing and broaching to, while they have to be realized, need never be experienced if you handle your boat with the attention she deserves. One last bit of advice on this question of broaching to. If your boat shows a continual tendency, when you are at sea, to broach to, lower the peak of the mainsail if she is gaff-rigged; if she is Bermuda-rigged, stop and tuck in a reef.

The third danger is rolling. If the yacht rolls violently she may get her boom in the water, with the same bad consequences as when broaching to. The antidotes to rolling are as follows: – Firstly, if your boat is a centreboard boat, and the centreboard is not already lowered, lower it. Secondly, haul in the main sheet a little. Boats of broad beam roll much more easily than narrow boats when running. The boom should always be topped up with the topping lift when running, as this helps to keep it out of the water.

Sailing with a quartering wind is much the same as sailing before the wind. There is, however, no danger in this instance of the accidental gybe or of rolling. But there still exists the danger of broaching to. This can be guarded against as usual by alert steering. When sailing with a quartering wind the mainsail is trimmed a little closer and the jib will draw instead of flapping idly in the lee of the mainsail. If the boat shows a strong tendency to broach to, the peak of the gaff should be lowered as when running. This manoeuvre of dropping the peak is called scandalizing. To complete the 'scandalizing' of the mainsail and further reduce sail area without reefing, pass a line through the highest reef cringle you can reach or over a mast hoop. Untie the tack lashing in the case of a loose-footed sail and trice it up to the cringle. If the foot of the sail is laced to the boom you cannot of course do this without unlacing it, which is not always practicable to do. In some cases where the boom is not secured to the mast by a gooseneck but has jaws like the gaff, you can trice up the boom without undoing the tack lashing. Generally speaking, though, dropping the peak should suffice. Remember that dropping the peak reduces the sail area aft of the centre of resistance of the boat, and when you alter course to sail the boat to windward you must hoist the peak first.

When you have become experienced at running, you can get the boat to sail faster by increasing your sail area by means of a spinnaker (see Fig. 31).

A spinnaker is a large, baggy, light, triangular-shaped sail. It is set on the side of the boat opposite the mainsail. It is what is called set flying. That is to say, it is secured to the boat at its three clews and not along any of its edges. The tack is secured to the outer end of a light spar which is attached to the mast near the mast band, and which is called the spinnaker boom. It is controlled by means of a line called the boom guy, which leads to the cockpit.

The clew is also sheeted aft. The spinnaker is not an easy sail to handle, especially in a quartering wind. If you are dead before the wind it is easier, so we will consider that first.

First of all, clear the spinnaker of any twists. Then with the boat sailing along, one hand goes forward and secures the head of the spinnaker to the spinnaker halliard. The spinnaker halliard is generally kept cleated to the mast ready for use. It should have a swivel-shackle and a snap hook that can be snapped into the becket (or loop) at the head of the spinnaker. The spinnaker boom is placed on the weather deck with the outboard end headed forward. The tack of the spinnaker is secured to the outboard end of the boom. The sheet which is fast to the clew is held by one member of the crew aft. The hand forward now passes the boom guy, which is secured to the boom's outer end, around outside the shrouds back to the cockpit. Now the helmsman belays the guy to a cleat and the hand forward begins to hoist on the halliard, and at the same time pushes the boom out over the bows and secures its inboard end to the mast either by a conical socket device or a small goose-neck, or, if the boom has jaws, by resting them against the mast. The spinnaker goes up. When it is high enough, the man hoisting makes fast to any convenient cleat, while the hand controlling the guy hauls the boom aft until it is at right angles to the boat. If there is much wind there will be a hard strain on the guy when the boom is pulled aft. When the boom is at right angles to the boat, the sail will be drawing and the guy can be belayed to a cleat. The sail is now kept drawing by the sheet hand who keeps his eyes glued to the sail, particularly the luff. As soon as this begins to shake and the sail shows signs of collapsing, he hauls in the sheet smartly until the sail is drawing again, while the guy hand eases away on the guy. As soon as the sail is drawing again the sheet is eased and the boom pulled aft once again.

As well as an after guy, a forward guy is useful, especially in a quartering wind, when the boom is headed forward of athwartships. The forward guy may be led forward through a block shackled to the deck, or just abaft the stem-head, and led aft to the cockpit. It can then be hauled on or slackened in conjunction with the guy and sheet. The helmsman's duty all the while is to steer the best course if he is racing. If cruising, he can steer to keep the spinnaker drawing, and the job of the guy and sheet hands becomes relatively easier. For illustration of the handling of a spinnaker see Fig. 32.

When you take in (hand) a spinnaker you just reverse the process of setting it. You send a hand forward. Then you slack off the guy, allowing the boom to go forward, spilling the wind out of the sail. The forward hand unships the inboard end of the boom and brings the boom carefully inboard. As soon as it is inboard, the clew and the tack are cast off and the sheet hand gathers in the foot of the sail in the lee of the mainsail. When he has done this, the forward hand lets go the halliard. As the sail comes down he makes the two ends of the halliard fast to their appropriate cleat and coils down the guy. The sail is bagged and returned to the sail locker. Some boats have a small topping lift and a downhaul fitted to the spinnaker boom (see Fig. 32). In very light airs the former helps to keep the sail drawing, while in strong breezes the tendency of the boom to fly up may be controlled by the downhaul. Although all this increases the amount of gear on the fo'c'sle, they are well worth the trouble, and make for efficient spinnaker work.

You will find in practice, particularly when you begin racing, that you seldom have a course directly down wind. You will most likely find that it is a quartering sea or a broad reach. In this instance the setting and trimming of a spinnaker is a little more difficult. The boom cannot be

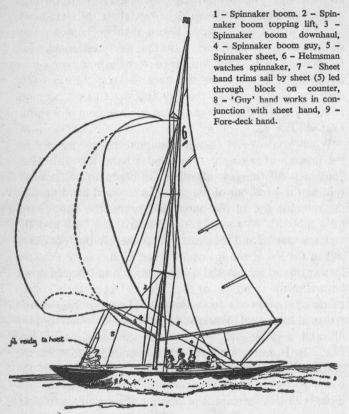

1 – Spinnaker boom. 2 – Spinnaker boom topping lift, 3 – Spinnaker boom downhaul, 4 – Spinnaker boom guy, 5 – Spinnaker sheet, 6 – Helmsman watches spinnaker, 7 – Sheet hand trims sail by sheet (5) led through block on counter, 8 – 'Guy' hand works in conjunction with sheet hand, 9 – Fore-deck hand.

jib ready to hoist

Fig. 32 – Spinnaker work.

In this sketch of a yacht running with her spinnaker set, the rigging, gear, and duties of crew are shown; the details may vary with different craft. The principles: a sheet and a guy to trim with, a downhaul to stop the boom flying up, a topping lift to prevent the boom sagging, and each member of the crew with his own particular job to do, remain the same.

guyed at right angles to the boat, because, if it is, the wind will blow on the forward side of the sail and slow down the boat. The boom will have to be considerably forward of the beam. Now as the boom is hauled aft from a fore-and-aft position, the sail will fill more quickly, and when it is allowed to go forward the sail will spill the wind less quickly. There is in point of fact less margin of safety between the sail being full of wind and straining, and empty of wind and able to be handled.

The boom should be well topped up with the topping lift, as this helps the mainsail to spill its wind into the spinnaker. When using a spinnaker the jib can be left hoisted, and you should try to trim your sails so that the spent wind of one sail is spilt into another. The mainsail should spill into the spinnaker and the spinnaker into the jib, thereby making the maximum use of all these sails. This kind of thing, however impossible it may sound, will assuredly come with practice and experience. One way of setting a spinnaker, which is often used on the larger ocean-racing yachts, is to set it in stops. This is both useful and quite fun to do.

First lay out the spinnaker on deck with the luff and the leech alongside each other. Roll up the centre part of the sail tightly. You should now have a long, thin sausage with the luff and leech together on the outside, and the clew and tack together at the bottom. Now take some ordinary cotton thread – do not use anything heavier – and tie the sail with a single turn of the thread at intervals of two feet or so. The sail, thus stopped, is then sent up the mast by the halliard and the foot made fast until the spinnaker is wanted. To break it out, make the sheet fast to a cleat and the tack fast to the outboard end of the boom. When the boom is secured to the mast and guyed aft the rest of the stops will go.

The advantage of setting a spinnaker in stops is that you

can break it out more easily and quickly than if you had to bend it on and hoist it. In racing, this time-saving factor is very important. When cruising, apart from the fun of watching the stops go as the sail fills, it has no very great advantage except on certain occasions when it may be useful to have the spinnaker ready waiting for an expected alteration of course that will need its employment.

In the large cruising and ocean-racing yachts, the setting of a spinnaker may be much simplified by reeving an out-haul through a sheave on the outboard end of the spinnaker boom. The boom, having been secured at its inboard end to the mast in the usual way, is kept horizontal by the topping lift (see Fig. 32 (2)) and is kept at right angles to the yacht's fore-and-aft line by being guyed aft with the guy (see Fig. 32 (4)). The spinnaker is then bent and hoisted, the tack being bent, not to the end of the boom, but to the outhaul. The spinnaker is now up and down the mast lying in the lee of the mainsail. Now haul away on the outhaul and the sail is set and may be trimmed with sheet and guy as usual. To lower the sail simply reverse the procedure of setting it. This method, which is particularly useful in large vessels and in vessels where the crew is very small, is advocated by Captain John Illingworth in his excellent book on 'offshore' racing.

So much for sailing before the wind. It is the least exciting point of sailing. The following wind denies you the thrill of the sensation of speed, and in actual fact, when running, a boat does not travel her fastest. Her own speed being in the same direction as the wind negatives the wind's impetus to a certain extent. The only type of craft that sail very fast when running are dinghies and other similarly designed craft. These craft, when they reach a certain speed, plane on the flat after-sections of their hull. They have centreboards which are raised when planing and the resis-tance caused by the friction of the wetted surface is enormously reduced. A dinghy when planing attains speeds far higher than when close-hauled, and this is a most exciting and satisfying sensation. It *is* possible for seagoing craft to plane. Light displacement craft can plane on the turn of their bilges under certain conditions when running down wind.

SEA SICKNESS

Most doctors agree that this is very largely a disorder of the nervous system. The amount of tolerance that training and familiarity with the sea will produce varies very much.

CONTRIBUTORY CAUSES IN ADDITION TO THE SEA'S MOTION:

Worry and apprehension, cold, fatigue, engine-room smells, general system out of order.

TREATMENT:

(1) *Prevention.*

Exercise, good general health, reasonable rest, absence of indigestion, warm clothes when needed, plenty of hot meals. (There are various anti-seasickness prescriptions on the market, one of the best of which is called Avomine, obtainable at most chemists.)

(2) *During Seasickness.*

(a) Mild Attack – Dry foods like biscuits and cold chicken; also glucose or barley sugar. Keep in the open if possible, with the wind in your face, and try and concentrate on work of some sort.

(b) Bad Attack – Lie down with head low, keep warm, eat dry foods as above, endeavour to remember that it can't last for ever.

'Nothing I like better than eating hot stewed steak in a southerly gale!'

CHAPTER 10

Reaching

—

A REACH can be defined as any course that is not directly before the wind, when the sails are not sheeted in hard. When the sails are trimmed fairly flat and the boat is almost close-hauled, the boat is said to be on a close reach. When the wind is abaft the beam, she is said to be on a broad reach (see Fig. 31).

Reaching is the fastest point of sailing, and while reaching the yacht makes less leeway than when close-hauled. To trim the sails correctly for a reach, as soon as the yacht is on her correct course, ease out the main sheet and head sheets until the luffs of the sails are beginning to shake. Then haul in on the sheets until they cease to shake and then haul in a little more to get the best trim. Now belay the sheets. Unless the wind shifts you can now sail on a landmark or compass bearing. You will be able to tell if the wind draws ahead or aft by watching the burgee, the sails, the direction of the waves, and by the feel of the ship when you have had more experience. To get the best out of your boat you should always study the wind's direction and trim your sheets accordingly. For example, if the wind draws ahead, the luffs of the sails will start to shake, and in order to trim the sheets correctly for the course you are sailing, you should haul them in until the luffs cease to shake. If, on the other hand the wind draws further aft, the yacht will be heeled over, but you will lose speed; the burgee will point further ahead and the feel of the wind on your face will be less. To trim the sheets correctly, ease them until the sail is making roughly the same angle with the

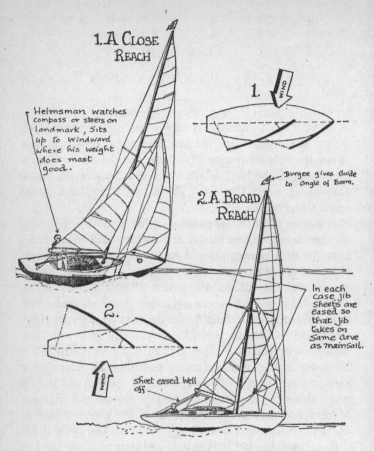

1. A CLOSE REACH

Helmsman watches compass or steers on landmark, sits up to windward where his weight does most good.

1.

WIND

Burgee gives guide to angle of boom.

2. A BROAD REACH

In each case jib sheets are eased so that jib takes on same curve as mainsail.

2.

WIND

Sheet eased well off

Reaching is fastest point of Sailing

Fig. 33 – Reaching.

ship's centre-line as the burgee. The burgee is always a good guide to the trim of the sails when reaching or sailing close-hauled. When reaching it is a mistake to pin the sheets in too hard. The sails should never be flat. If you do this you will waste wind and increase leeway. The yacht will heel over with water pouring along the lee rail, but as we saw when the wind shifted aft while we were reaching, speed is lost, both on account of the wastage of wind caused by incorrect trimming of the sails, and on account of the extra friction caused by the immersion of the ship's top strake and rail in the water.

To get a yacht to sail at her best you must pay careful attention to this question of trim. If you have to hold the tiller very slightly 'up' or towards the wind, the vessel is said to carry 'weather helm'. Most yachts are designed to carry a little 'weather helm', as it is easier to steer a yacht to windward if she has a slight pressure on the tiller. It is also advisable to have weather helm because it increases the aerodynamic or, in this case, hydrodynamic efficiency. By fixing the rudder at a small angle to leeward, the combination of the boat's keel and rudder becomes a more effective hydrofoil (like an aerofoil or aeroplane's wing).

However, if your yacht appears to have too much weather helm, and you find that you have to hold the tiller well up to windward to get her to hold her course, this is in all probability because the main sheet is hauled in too hard. The yacht pivots about a point somewhere near the mast, for argument's sake, and if the pressure on the mainsail is too great owing to its being sheeted in too hard, it will be clear that the yacht's stern will tend to swing away from the wind and her bows to swing into the wind. In other words, weather helm.

To cure this excess of weather helm is simple. Just ease the main sheet! If the jib is sheeted in too hard, you will notice the mainsail 'lifting' along the luff. When this happens, ease out the jib sheet until the jib is taking up about the same curve as the mainsail.

I shall have more to say on this question of trim in Chapter 13, so I will not go into it any more here. We will now consider windward sailing, the most exhilarating of all points of sailing, especially in a good breeze.

SHENANDOA

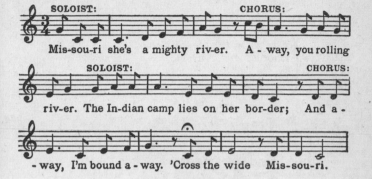

Mis-sou-ri she's a mighty riv-er. A - way, you rolling riv-er. The In-dian camp lies on her bor-der; And a - way, I'm bound a - way. 'Cross the wide Mis-sou-ri.

O, Shenandoa! I love your daughter,
Chorus: A-way, you rolling river.
I'll take her 'cross you rolling water,
Chorus: And away, we're bound away,
'Cross the wide Missouri

The Chief refused the white man's offer,
Chorus: A-way, you rolling river;
And vowed the white man should not have her,
Chorus: And away, etc.

One day a ship sailed up the river,
Chorus: A-way, etc.
And brought the Chief the strong fire-water
Chorus: And away, etc.

With Yankee notions she was laden,
Chorus: A-way, etc.
Her Captain loved the Indian maiden,
Chorus: And away, etc.

He made the Chief drunk with fire-water,
  Chorus: *A-way,* etc.
And 'cross the river stole the daughter
  Chorus: *And away,* etc.

O, Shenandoa! I long to hear you,
  Chorus: *A-way you rolling river;*
Across the wide and rolling river,
  Chorus: *And away,* etc.

CHAPTER 11

Close-Hauled

—

THE golden rule, when sailing to windward, is: Don't starve the ship. This means: never pin the sails so hard that the boat becomes sluggish, and never sail so close to the wind that the sails shiver and cease to drive the boat through the water. You will often think, when sailing to windward in company with other yachts, that they are pointing closer to the wind than you are. This is a common impression and nearly always a wrong one. And although the natural thing is to try and get your boat to point as high (close to the wind) as the other boats seem to be pointing, you must never do this. If you do your vessel will only lose speed. When sailing close-hauled you will find, if your boat is reasonably well-rigged, that you can pin the sheets in and make her point about 3 points off the wind (that is 33¾°, see Chapter 16), but she won't sail fast. If you 'free her' a point and sail 45° she will sail along nicely and you will get much farther to windward in a given time.

The whole object in windward sailing is to sail as close to the wind as possible without stopping the boat's way. Instead of sailing on a mark or by the compass as when reaching, you trim the sails as flat as will make the boat give the best performance (some sails can be trimmed flatter than others; experience will show you), and you meet the wind's vagaries by slight alterations of course. You fence with the wind by using the tiller. Thus if the wind draws ahead, the luffs of the sails will shake or lift and you must put the tiller 'up' (to windward), then turn the boat away from the wind to bring the wind more on the beam until the sails fill again. You must watch the luff of the sail and the burgee, or you can sit down to leeward like a racing helmsman and watch the leech of the jib. This is considered by many to be the best method (scc Fig. 34). When you see the burgee is making a broader angle with the boat than the sail, this is your warning that you are not sailing close enough. You must then put the helm 'down' (away from the wind) and bring the bows up into the wind until the luff starts to shake, then bear away just enough to put the luff to sleep again. Constant attention is needed to get the most out of a boat when close-hauled. Sailing a dinghy is excellent practice for this, because a dinghy's reactions are very quick and it teaches you to be alert, and to become accustomed to continual little alterations of course to make the boat point always as close to the wind as possible.

Trimming the sails to sail to windward is largely a matter of knowing the boat. Some vessels like being sheeted in hard, others, generally of a less 'racy' type, will not stand such hard sheeting. To begin with, trim the main sheet so that the end of the boom is just over the lee quarter, that is to say, the lee corner of the stern, and the jib sheet not quite as hard in as you can get it. The harder it is blowing the harder you can pin in the sheets. To pin them in hard in light airs will 'kill the boat's way'.

When sailing close-hauled, there is certain to be some leeway being made, and you must take advantage of every little strong puff of the wind to get back a little to windward. As soon as the puff comes and the yacht heels to it, ease the helm down very gently and let the yacht sail closer to the wind; as the puff dies down, the luff of the mainsail and the beck of the jib will begin to lift and quiver and you must bear away again to 'put them to sleep'. In this way you can make the boat 'eat out' to windward and save a surprising amount of ground, thereby cancelling or helping to cancel out your leeway.

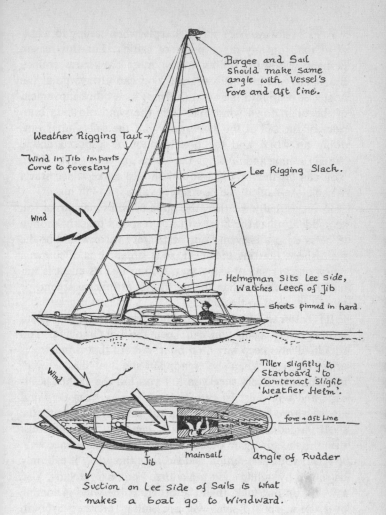

Burgee and Sail should make same angle with Vessel's Fore and Aft line.

Weather Rigging Taut →

Wind in Jib imparts Curve to forestay

Lee Rigging Slack.

Wind

Helmsman sits Lee side, watches Leech of Jib

sheets pinned in hard.

Tiller slightly to Starboard to counteract slight 'Weather Helm'.

Wind

fore + aft Line

Jib   Mainsail   Angle of Rudder

Suction on Lee side of Sails is what makes a boat go to Windward.

Fig. 34 – Close-hauled.

A yacht always heels more sharply when sailing to windward than on any other point of sailing. For this reason perhaps windward sailing is the most dangerous course. But it has one great advantage. You can always point the boat's bow up into the wind (luff up) by a quick movement of the tiller down wind. This lets the wind blow on both sides of the sail at the same time and the sails flutter out, doing no work, and the boat cannot be knocked down. When running and reaching the sheets are your safety valve. You can let them fly if a squall should make it necessary. When close-hauled, the best safety valve is to luff up.

In very squally weather, the puffs of wind may strike you so suddenly that the boat will not respond quickly enough to be safe; in this event your best safety valve would be the main sheet. Starting the sheet, as it is called, is of course a much quicker safety valve than luffing up. Its effect is immediate, whereas, when luffing, the boat takes a second or two to respond to the helm.

It is better to luff than to start the sheet, as by luffing up and bearing away again you can keep the boat moving. You should always keep way on a boat. A boat that is moving is under control. When she is stopped she is at the mercy of the elements. Every time you luff you kill the yacht's headway, and you must be careful to sail away from the wind again, before headway is lost. In the same way, starting the sheet immediately kills the boat's headway and you must trim the sheet in again quickly before you lose steerage way.

When your destination is dead into the wind, it can only be gained by sailing a zig-zag course known as tacking. You sail first on one tack, then the other. If the wind is coming over the starboard side, you are sailing on the starboard tack. If vice versa, you are on the port tack.

The origin of the expression dates, like so many others, from the days of the square-riggers. The two lower corners or clews of the sails each had a sheet leading aft and a tack leading forward. When the wind was forward of the beam, the weather tack was hauled aboard to make the sail take up an angle with the wind something like the angle of your yacht's mainsail when reaching. Thus when the wind was blowing over the starboard side, the starboard tacks were hauled aboard, and the ship was said to be sailing 'on the starboard tack'.

If it is thought that the objective can be reached in two tacks, continue on the first until the objective is well away on the weather quarter, that is, well over 90° from your present course. This is because, although your next course will point approximately 90° from your present one, the effect of leeway will surprise you. You should try to have the objective well on the lee bow after you have tacked. It is not difficult to go from one tack to the other. The yacht must have plenty of way on her. Just before reaching the end of a tack, or board as it is called, warn everyone on board by calling out 'Ready about!' When ready to turn call out 'lee oh!' Put the helm down. The yacht will turn up rapidly into the wind. As the wind comes on the other bow, the jib will be 'taken aback' and will help to push the boat's bows round to the new tack. Let fly the jib sheet. Meanwhile the mainsail will fill on the new tack, and the boom will swing smartly over. The jib should then be sheeted for the new tack and the helm steadied (see Fig. 35). You will have to ease the *new* lee runner and set up the *new* weather one. You will be able to work out a routine for doing this (see Fig. 35), but always get the new weather runner set up *before* the strain comes on it. It must be done, otherwise the lee runner will cut into the belly of the sail, and the mast will not be properly stayed against the pull of the sails. When sailing in heavy weather or a steep sea the action of the waves tends to make a boat sluggish. When coming about, choose a calm patch (a 'smooth') and always have plenty of way on the boat.

As in every other part of sailing there are two ways of going about – a right way and a wrong way. The right way is to ease the boat gently round and then while she has steerage way push the helm down sufficiently hard to bring her on to her new tack. In this way you lose no time and actually gain something in so far as you have carried the

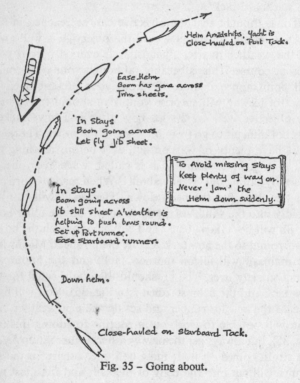

Helm Amidships, Yacht is Close-hauled on Port Tack.

Ease Helm Boom has gone across Trim sheets.

'In Stays' Boom going across Let fly jib sheet.

WIND

'In stays' Boom going across Jib still sheet A'weather is helping to push bows round. Set up Port runner. Ease Starboard runner.

To Avoid missing Stays Keep plenty of way on. Never 'Jam' the Helm down suddenly.

Down helm.

Close-hauled on Starboard Tack.

Fig. 35 – Going about.

boat some way into the wind. This movement ahead while actually going about is one of the hallmarks of a good windward helmsman. It is known as 'fore-reaching'.

The wrong way is to jam the helm suddenly down, and spin the boat round so far on to the other tack that you cannot

Plate 1. A smart little cruiser, up-to-date in every respect, entering harbour under mainsail. With a boat like this, you can potter, or race or cruise, and have the wonderful freedom of the seas.

Plate 2. A popular type of small family cruiser/racer.
South Coast One Design yachts under mainsail and spinnaker.

Plate 3. Gull's view of a dinghy – an 'Enterprise' from aloft.
The crew holds the jib to starboard and the
main boom to port, running in light airs.

Plate 4. A 'swarm' of Fireflies – a popular class of 12-foot racing dinghy, designed by Uffa Fox.

Plate 5. In modern times the famous America's Cup is raced
for in yachts of the 12-metre class. This is a 12-metre.
Note her spinnaker, and her headsail set in stops, ready
to break out.

Plate 7. *Prospect of Whitby* – a successful international off-shore
racer and member of the British team for Admiral's Cup races.

Plate 6. *Endeavour* – the famous British 'America's Cup'
challenger, designed by Charles Nicholson.

Plate 8. *Attempt* – an old ketch-rigged sailing barge of the 1890s. Note the loose-footed sails.

Plate 9. An 'International Dragon'. One of this very popular class which originated in Norway, designed by Johan Anker.

Plate 10. There is a wide variety of small cruisers available today, capable of taking part in races, like these two, shown competing for the Captain James Cook Trophy.

Plate 11. A modern ocean-racing yawl: strong, supremely seaworthy, and fast.

Plate 13. *Jem II* – one of the 'Star' Class, a very popular class in the U.S.A.

Plate 12. A dinghy of the 505 class. Note use of trapeze by crew to increase stability.

Plate 14. *Creole* – a beautiful 3-masted
fore-and-aft staysail schooner.

Plate 15. 'The poetry of motion that is sailing' – a fine photograph of *Endeavour*'s lee bow as she thunders past on the starboard tack.

Plate 16. *Jolie Brise* – a converted pilot cutter. The most famous of the pioneers of modern English ocean racing.

luff readily. It is very bad to carry the boat right off the wind and have to bring her back on to her course. If on the other hand you don't put the helm over enough, or have not enough way on, you may get 'caught in stays' (see Fig. 35). This means that the boat hangs pointing directly into the wind, with the wind blowing on both sides of the sails. You will at once lose headway and you will not be able to complete the tack. If this happens, there is only one thing to do. We will assume that you are on the port tack. You come to the end of a 'board' and start to go about. You cry 'ready about' and then 'lee oh!' and put the helm down. The boat goes up into the wind, but you did not have enough way on her. She hangs there, then begins to drift slowly backwards. What can you do? This has of course happened right in front of the club house of the yacht club you have newly joined and the members of which you are doing your utmost to impress. Your yacht's drifting ignominiously and helplessly astern is the signal for – horror of horrors! – the commodore to train his binoculars upon you. Now, if you have read this chapter carefully, is your chance!

Preserving an outward appearance of calm, you should act as follows:

First, put the tiller to port – not to starboard, mind – and sheet the jib to starboard. In a minute you will swing past the dead centre of the wind and will get the wind over the starboard bow. Now this is where you want it. As soon as this happens, put the tiller to starboard and in a moment you will have steerage way. The commodore will drop his glasses with a grunt of nautical approval and your pulse will go back to normal.

Now what has happened? While you were hanging in stays, your boat was not moving ahead. If it were you would have had sufficient steerage way to swing past the dead centre on to the starboard tack. But the boat had started to drift backwards. Now as soon as this happens, the action of the rudder is reversed. The water is flowing from the aft end of the rudder towards the forward end. Therefore to make the bow turn to port, you push the tiller to port, bringing the rudder to starboard. Similarly, by trimming the jib sheet and holding the boom amidships or slightly to starboard, you give the wind a chance to drive the bow round to port. Always remember when sailing against the wind that the minute your boat is not going ahead, it will begin to go astern. And when it is going astern, the action of the rudder is reversed.

When and if you come to take part in racing, whether offshore or in sheltered waters, you will without doubt make the acquaintance of the Genoa jib. This sail, probably the most useful of all racing headsails, is a large jib that overlaps the mainsail by about one third of its width (see Fig. 36). It can be carried on a reach and is very effective on that point of sailing, but its primary use is for going to windward. The Genoa jib helps to increase the aerofoil effect of the mainsail. It is primarily a racing sail, as it is a great nuisance when going about. When tacking in a large yacht, the lee sheet must be cast off and a hand must go forward to carry the jib round the windward shrouds, the mast, and the leeward shrouds. In a small racing yacht, the Genoa must be cased round the mast and shrouds by the sheet. Efficient handling of a Genoa jib is entirely a matter of practice.

But although a nuisance when cruising to windward, when holding a course for any length of time the Genoa pays dividends. With it you can point as close as and at times closer than with any other headsail, and it is, as we have said, remarkably efficient. To get it set properly, it must be sheeted in hard, and this puts a big strain on the mast and the hull. You should never put a Genoa on a boat that is unsuitable. The hull must be strongly built, and the stay on which the sail is set and the corresponding back stay must be strong. It is often set on the forestay, although the mod-

ern tendency is to set it on either the fore-topmast stay or a
stay running from the stem-head to a point a short distance

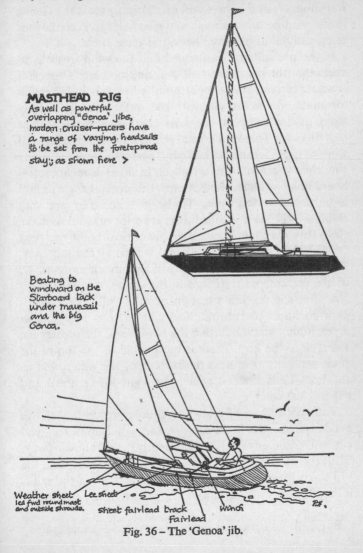

MASTHEAD RIG
As well as powerful
overlapping "Genoa' jibs,
modern cruiser-racers have
a range of varying headsails
to be set from the foretopmast
stay; as shown here >

Beating to
windward on the
Starboard tack
under mainsail
and the big
Genoa.

Weather sheet   Lee sheet
led fwd round mast
and outside shrouds.   Sheet fairlead track   Winch
                                        Fairlead
                      Fig. 36 – The 'Genoa' jib.

below the mast-head. Use of the fore-topmast stay for all jibs is common nowadays. When using the Genoa on a reach you should lead the sheet well aft. This prevents the Genoa 'back-winding' the mainsail, and also helps to keep the foot of the sail out of the water when the yacht heels.

If you are sailing close-hauled and the wind freshens so much that the boat heels well over and becomes sluggish it is wisest to reef. It is a moot point when a boat is heeling too much. Some are safe with the water running happily along the lee scuppers, but most boats do not sail at their best this way. There is a critical point, known as the 'critical angle of heel', when a vessel finds it easier to keep on turning over than to return to an even keel. In shoal draught centre-board boats, with flattish bottoms, this critical angle of heel is particularly noticeable. To begin with, they are very stable – 'stiff' as it is called. It takes a lot of wind to make them lean over much, but after the critical point has been reached they have no stability and will go all the way over. On the other hand a keel boat will lean much more easily, as she presents no resistance in the shape of a hard bilge, but after she reaches a certain point it will take a hurri-cane to knock her down. The lead or iron keel acts as a pendulum, and the further the boat heels, the greater the leverage of the keel. There is more wind at the top of the mast generally than near the surface of the water, and as the boat heels her sail area is brought lower down and catches less wind.

With both types of craft you should reef before things get dangerous. But if, for some reason, you cannot reef, you can sail reasonably safely and efficiently in the following way. Trim the jib sheet in flat; ease off the main sheet until the sail starts lifting. Continue until about a third of the sail is lifting. In this way you can sail surprisingly fast and safely.

But until you become really expert, close-hauled sailing

is very much a full-time job. It is only by taking advantage of every little puff and reacting to every shift of wind, that you will 'get there'. And when you have learnt how to make your boat go to windward well, there are few more exciting and satisfying feelings.

Yes, the rewards of windward sailing are many. To feel the sting of the spray in your face; to hear the sound of the bows clipping the water and the music of the sea foaming past the lee rail; to feel in perfect command of your vessel and to see her steadily overhauling her opponents in a race – all these and many other wonderful things are the reward of practice.

We have learnt how to sail before the wind and on the wind. Let us now consider how to anchor and how to pick up the moorings we laid in Chapter 4.

ONE DAY IN MAY

(The kind of weather every prospective yacht owner visualizes, – but seldom sees!)

We slip our moorings in the Hamble river and proceed slowly down river. The tide is fair, but as yet is not running very fast, and what little wind there is is fluky and erratic. But all the same we make good progress, and soon Bursledon is far astern and we are turning the corner by the water tower that rears itself up to starboard – a well-known landmark to all who know the Hamble.

It is still early, for we rose early in order to catch the tide, and as yet the sun is not shining with its full strength; but as the wind increases to a pleasant sailing breeze, the feel of the sun on our faces grows warmer and warmer, and we know with certainty that it is going to be another wonderfully fine day. Now we are threading our way round the mass of craft that lie moored in midstream near Warsash and the river mouth. We are close-hauled, and with the tide now running more strongly under us, we have to tack carefully to avoid being carried by it on to one of the hundreds of moored yachts. It is Saturday and most of the owners are already aboard, indeed many have slept on board and are now preparing to get under way, busily engaged in the hundred and one little jobs that are so necessary and at the same time seem so trivial to the man – unhappy creature that he is – who doesn't sail.

Now we are entering Southampton Water and we can see our objective, Cowes, over to port. The sky is clear and cloudless, and across its unbelievably bright expanse hundreds of gulls glide and turn, filling the air with their cries. We pass Calshot Castle to starboard. We take two short legs and a long one and then square off for Cowes. Now we can see Saunders Roe's white building and Cowes Castle and the Green. There are several yachts anchored in the Roads but it is not too crowded. It is still early in the season and the only people sailing at this time of year are those who love sailing for its own sake. Now we are in the Roads. There's that new Nicholson we saw in the Hamble the other week-end, and there's old so and so, and there's the ferry just leaving, and what a lot of people there are on shore.

Here we are then, down headsail, up into the wind, a pause and then splash followed by the merry clatter of the cable running out. The cable is snubbed at twelve fathoms: that should be enough here. We stow the sails, leisurely drinking in the scene and the hot sun. At this moment there is no one on earth with whom we would change places . . .

THIRTY SQUARE METRES

CHAPTER 12

Anchoring, Picking Up Moorings, and Stowing Ship

—

WE have learned the principles of weighing anchor and of leaving moorings. We have got our ship under way and we have sailed her on all points of sailing. Now the time has come to anchor. We will assume that you have been for a short day cruise and have arrived at the harbour of your destination.

Now there are certain things which must be done. Firstly, if you are entering a strange harbour have a very good look at the chart (see Chapter 16 for information about charts). Notice the depths of water shown and the general layout of the harbour. There will probably be other vessels at anchor and this will give you a good guide.

Get the anchor ready. It may be unstocked, that is, the stock (see Fig. 9) may be lying alongside the shank instead of at right angles to it. Push the stock into place and secure it by driving the pin provided well home. Range a fathom or so of cable on deck and make certain the cable can run easily through the chain pipe or navel pipe. On the chart you will have observed the depth of water (see Tides, Chapter 16). Let us suppose that there are three fathoms where you intend to bring up. You will have to veer at least nine fathoms then. The amount of cable should equal 3 or 4 times the depth at high water, and more if it blows hard. We will assume then that you have selected for your anchorage a place reasonably near the shore, reasonably sheltered with room to swing without endangering other yachts in the vicinity, and in 3 fathoms of water at high tide. If your cable is marked, as it should be, you will be able to tell how much cable you veer (let out). From the chart you have observed what the tide is doing in the harbour, and you have led the cable through the fairlead in the bows and back inboard where it is shackled on to the anchor. All you have to do now is to throw the anchor clear over the side and the cable will run out after it. But we are not quite ready yet. There are some important factors to be considered. How are you going to approach the anchorage and what tactics will you use? These are some rules for anchoring which can be memorized:

(1) When there is no tide:
    (a) Luff head to wind.
    (b) Lower headsails.
    (c) Wait till the yacht gathers sternway.
    (d) Let go the anchor.

(2) When the wind and tide are in the same direction and yacht is *close-hauled*:
Same as for (1).

(3) When wind and tide are in the same direction and yacht is *running*:
    (a) Lower mainsail and approach under headsails.
    (b) Lower headsails a little way from the chosen spot.
    (c) Let go the anchor.
    (d) Snub (stop running out) the cable and allow the yacht to swing to the tide.

(4) When wind is against tide (yacht will be *running**):
    (a) Lower mainsail and approach under headsails.
    (b) Just before reaching anchorage lower headsails.
    (c) Wait till yacht gathers sternway.
    (d) Let go the anchor.

Let us assume that the wind and tide are in the same direction and the yacht is close-hauled. Sail up to the selected anchorage and then luff up head to wind. Lower the jib. The

* It is best to anchor against the tide

yacht will move ahead gradually losing way (you will learn by experience how far your own boat carries her way) and will come to a dead stop. She will then begin to drift astern. The rapidity with which she loses way and starts to drift astern depends of course on the strength of the wind and the rate of the tide. When she begins to drift astern, heave over the anchor. If you have an anchor winch, you will be able to control the amount of cable you veer. If you have not, you can easily control its headlong rush by standing on it. Watch the white marks on the cable and count the number of fathoms being veered. The reason that you must have sternway on the boat before letting go is because if you let go while the boat is stopped the cable will fall on top of the anchor and a coil may catch round one of the flukes, thus causing the anchor to drag. Do not veer all the cable at once, but veer gradually. When you are satisfied that the anchor is holding and not dragging, you can lower and stow your mainsail.

If you are uncertain of the depth of water in which you are about to anchor, take a sounding with the lead line. This is an invaluable piece of gear which you should never be without. To heave it, take the lead with about three or four foot of line in your hand. Make sure the line is free to run easily over the side, and swing the lead well ahead of the ship. The line will run out through your hand and as it comes perpendicular you will be able to feel it touch the bottom. Notice the nearest marker above the water level and this will give you the depth. If the depth corresponds with any of the marks on the line, this is called 'by the mark 5', 'by the mark 7'. If it corresponds with one of the deeps, that is called 'deep 6', 'deep 8', etc. If a quarter or a half a fathom more than a mark or deep, that is called 'and a quarter 7', 'and a quarter 8', etc. If less than a mark or deep, it will be 'a quarter less 7', etc. (see Fig. 37). A lead line should be made of sennit or plaited line that does not twist. Window sash cord makes an excellent cheap substitute.

As an insurance against your anchor dragging, note down the bearings of three conspicuous objects. But with regard to dragging, if you are going to remain long at anchor, you should moor with the kedge. A yacht at single anchor in a tideway is not secure. Sooner or later, when the tide turns she will ride over her anchor and foul it (see Fig. 9). Then, when it blows she will drag.

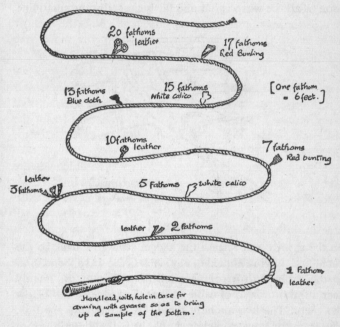

Fig. 37 – How the 'Lead Line' is marked. The intermediate depths (4, 6, 8, 9, 11, 12, 14, 16, and 18 fathoms) are known as 'deeps' and are estimated by reference to the nearest 'mark'.

To moor with the kedge, anchor in the usual way, having beforehand bent one end of the kedge warp on to the ring of the kedge anchor with a round turn and two half hitches or a bowline (see Chapter 5). Having veered the necessary amount of cable, make one end of the kedge warp fast on the fo'c'sle and put the coil of the warp into the dinghy near the transom, with the anchor lying right in the stern. Capsize the coil so that as you row away from the yacht the warp will pay out. Now place the anchor over the dinghy's stern and secure it there by a short piece of line passing through the ring of the anchor and made fast to the thwart by means of a slippery hitch (see Fig. 38). Row astern, and as soon as all the warp is out and fairly taut, slip the small line

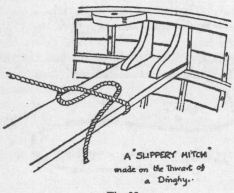

A "SLIPPERY HITCH"
made on the Thwart of
a Dinghy.

Fig. 38

on the thwart and release the kedge. Now row back to the yacht and, having hauled in any slack in the warp, bend it on to the cable with a rolling hitch (see Chapter 5). Finally veer a fathom or so of cable so that the kedge is well below the yacht. The two anchors should lie in line with the tide. The main (or bower) anchor should lie in the direction from which the greatest strain will come. For example if you were anchoring in a creek open to the sea, you would have the bower anchor towards the mouth of the creek: if you were anchoring in a river with a strong ebb you would have the bower anchor up river. If you have to anchor overnight in an open anchorage like the creek mentioned above, always have everything ready for weighing anchor, before turning in, so that if the wind gets up during the night you can get under way and out of danger as quickly as possible. Dragging your anchor on to a lee shore is a very unpleasant experience. If possible always select an anchorage that is sheltered from the prevailing wind.

It is perfectly possible to moor with two anchors without using the dinghy at all. If the wind and tide are in the same direction, you luff head to wind, let go the bower anchor and drop astern veering cable. You veer twice the amount of cable required for the depth of water, that is to say, in 3 fathoms veer 18 and not 9. Then let go the kedge and haul back on the bower anchor's cable, easing out the kedge warp until you are midway between the two. Bend the warp to the cable with a rolling hitch as before, then veer out the cable so that the place where the two join is well under the yacht, and the yacht can swing freely.

If the wind is against the tide, you let go the bower anchor and, slacking away on it, carry on against the tide under jib for twice the amount of cable required. Then let go the kedge, lower the jib, and drift back on the tide, hauling in the cable and veering the kedge warp until the yacht is midway between the two. Once again, to prevent the kedge warp and the anchor chain fouling each other when the yacht swings with the tide, bend the warp to the cable with a rolling hitch as soon as the yacht is middled. You should then veer out the cable so that the yacht can swing freely.

A yacht at anchor rides to the weight of cable rather than the anchor itself. If it really blows up, however, and the sea rises, she may start snubbing, that is, bringing the cable up taut as she pitches. If this happens, you can help the yacht greatly (and very possibly save the cable) by attaching a pig of lead or iron ballast to the cable by means of a large shackle which you can buy at any yacht chandler's. The pig should have a light line bent to it by means of which it can be lowered well down the cable. It will act as a buffer and will take the jar off the cable, because before the cable can snub taut it must carry the weight of the ballast, and before it can do that the wave will have passed, and the cable will sag once more under the weight.

If, on arrival at a new harbour, you see a lot of mooring buoys, do not anchor in their vicinity. If there is no stretch of suitable water well clear of these, it is better to ask permission to pick up a vacant buoy. The reason is that where moorings are laid for yachts year after year, the whole sea bed will be literally strewn with old moorings, old ground chain, and the unmarked chains of existing moorings. A stranger anchoring in or near such places is all too likely to get his anchor caught in the tangle. This is called a foul anchor, and there are two remedies. One, and by far the best, is, on those occasions where the nature of the bottom is in doubt, to buoy the anchor. The buoy rope should be more than long enough to reach from the surface to the bottom at high water and should be strong enough to weigh the anchor. The lower end should be bent to the *crown* of the anchor with a clove hitch (see Chapter 5) and the upper end to the strop of a small buoy. If, on weighing, the anchor will not come home, one good tug at the buoy will generally free it. If under force of circumstances you have to ditch anchor and cable (a most unfortunate occurrence!) the buoy will act as a marker for later salvage operations. The second method is an emergency method. Heave up on the anchor chain as much as you can, lifting the chain in which the anchor is caught off the bottom. Heave it as high as you can and make fast. Now try to reach the mooring chain with the boat hook. If you cannot, lash an oar to it and try again. Next get the lead line and drop the lead ahead of the mooring chain and fish it up the other side, using the boat hook. Now bend a stout warp to the lead line and haul it under the mooring chain and back inboard. Haul it taut and make fast. Then slacken away the cable so that the weight of the mooring chain is taken by the warp, and continue until the anchor drops clear of the mooring chain. You can now clear the anchor easily, and when you want to get under way all you have to do is to slip the warp.

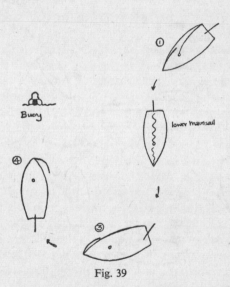

Fig. 39

So much then for anchoring. We can now come to the question of picking up permanent moorings in harbour. Suppose you are beating to windward with a fair tide (see Fig. 39). You sail past the mooring, lower mainsail, and run back to the buoy under jib, which you furl just before reaching it. If you have judged it correctly (and this is largely a matter of knowing your vessel) the yacht will lose way just as she comes up to the buoy.

If the wind is on the beam, and the tide is fair, you do exactly the same, but you must get to windward of the buoy before lowering mainsail so that you can easily get back under the jib (see Fig. 40).

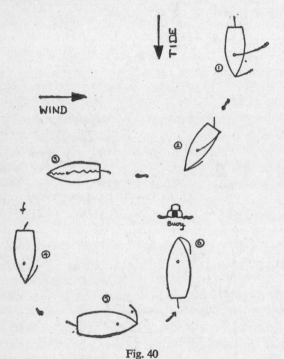

Fig. 40

If you are beating against a foul tide, you beat up to the buoy and luff on to it and lower the headsail.

If you are reaching against a foul tide, lower the jib and luff on to the buoy, and as soon as you have the buoy safely aboard let the main sheet run so that there will be no wind in the mainsail.

Finally if you are running with a fair tide, you must round the vessel up to the buoy. This is the hardest of all, as you must estimate the strength of the tide and set it against the amount of way your yacht carries.

It is all largely a matter of knowing your boat and being able to judge the tide's strength correctly, and you cannot practise it too often. Being able to round up alongside an object in the water may one day save the life of someone who has fallen overboard!

If you actually do lose a man overboard, throw him a lifebuoy and then gybe. No matter on what point of sailing you are on, gybe. The yacht must pick him up when she has little or no way on her and is head to wind. Consequently you must approach from leeward. The quickest way to get the yacht into this position is to gybe.

When you have anchored (or secured to a mooring) you should then 'stow ship'. Ease down the boom on the topping lift until it rests in its crutch. Haul in the main sheet to keep the boom in a secure position. (If you have loose crutches there is generally a small piece of line bent on to the crutches to pass over the boom to hold it down.) Now haul the mainsail across the boom so that it lies all on one side. Then take hold of the leech and take it forward along the boom, letting it overlap a little – say a foot or two. Lean across the boom and gather up the belly of the sail evenly and shake it down inside itself. Repeat this procedure, taking a fresh grip on the sail each time farther down than the last, until the whole sail has been smoothed into a sausage inside a tight skin. Smooth all wrinkles out of this skin and secure it to the boom with thin strips of canvas known as gaskets or tiers. Most yachts have a canvas 'coat' that laces over the boom and covers the mainsail.

The next thing to do is to put the headsail or headsails into their respective sail bags and stow them away. Of course if the mainsail and headsails are at all wet you should *not* furl or bag them, but, if it is not raining, should hoist them and let them dry first. If it is raining, stow them but do not coat the mainsail, and hoist and dry them all at the first opportunity.

Having finished with the sails, belay all halliards round their proper cleats and coil down the ends. Then, to prevent them beating a tattoo on the mast when it blows, either secure them to the main shrouds with thin line, or twist one of them, say the main halliard, round the mast and then belay it to its cleat. At sunset, the ensign and burgee should be hauled down and an anchor light hoisted. The best place is on the forestay. Shackle the handle of the lamp at the top to the forestay by means of an ordinary 'D' shackle and also shackle the jib halliard to the same handle. The lamp can now be hoisted a little way up the forestay by means of the jib halliard. If the yacht is likely to roll the lamp can be kept steady by leading two lanyards, one from each side of the base of the lamp down to a small cleat or ring-bolt each side of the fo'c'sle.

You will, at some time or other, have to moor alongside another yacht or a jetty. In this event have every available fender handy on deck. Everything should be ready, a warp coiled down for'ard and another warp coiled down aft. Come alongside against the stream when possible and with as little way on as you can. Get the bow warp out as quickly as possible, and as soon as this is made fast ashore or aboard the other vessel, the yacht can be allowed to drop back on the tide while the stern warp is made fast. If you have moored alongside another yacht the rise and fall of the tide will not trouble you, but if you are alongside a quay wall, the longer your head rope and stern rope and the further apart on the shore, the better, because the rise and fall will make much less difference than if they were close together. Where there is no tide, head and stern warps backed up by shorter lines at the bow and quarter will be sufficient (see Fig. 41) but where there is any stream running, you will have to put out 'springs'.

Lead a warp from the inboard bow to a cleat or bollard ashore well abaft the beam, and another warp from the inboard quarter to a bollard well ahead. By adjusting the strain on these springs, as they are called, you can keep the yacht well in position however hard the stream may be running.

If you are lying alongside a quay which is faced with big baulks of timber that jut out from the side of the quay wall, you will find it practically impossible to keep your fenders resting against them. They will soon slip out of place. The

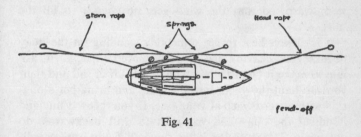

Fig. 41

best thing is to sling a spare spar, like a sweep or spinnaker boom, over the side, outside the fenders and resting against them. In this way it will take the chafe and the fenders will prevent the spar from damaging the ship's side.

The technique of coming alongside or leaving a quay is one which you can learn only by experience. Never try to do it with a strange boat until you know how far she will 'shoot'. By shooting I mean bringing the yacht up into the wind from such a direction and in such a way that she will lose all headway and come to a standstill just as you reach the quay.

Suppose that the wind is blowing directly off a quay. In this case, the best method of approaching it is on a close reach. Then, timing it so that the yacht will be heading into the wind when she is to leeward of the quayside, and trimming the sheets gradually, you put the helm down, luff into the wind and head directly up wind towards the quay. If you have timed it correctly, the yacht will stop before she reaches the quay. If you are going too fast, fend off with a boat hook from the bows. As the yacht comes to a stop you throw a heaving line (or your warp if it is not too large), or if there is no one on the quay one of the crew should jump ashore and make fast the bow line. Once secured, lower sail quickly. A yacht behaves quite well at a quay with sails set provided she is pointing head to wind, but you must lower sail before heaving the yacht's stern round with the stern warp, so that the wind gets no chance to fill the sails.

It is always best to get somebody standing on the quay to take your heaving line or warp. Once he has got it, ask him to make it fast to a nearby bollard; lower sail and then you can haul the yacht into the quay and bring her alongside with a stern warp at your ease. If you throw a line and it misses the quay and you start to drift backwards, do not panic. The situation is the same as if you were caught in stays. Remember that the action of the rudder is reversed. The wisest thing is to sail away from the quay and try again.

If the wind is blowing directly on to the quay face, the problem is rather harder. One way is to sail as close to the quay as you can, luff up, and anchor. You can then lower sail and ease out on the cable slowly until the yacht's stern is almost touching the quay, when you can easily get your warps ashore and bring the yacht alongside without doing her any damage.

But if possible always moor on the *lee* side of a quay. However many fenders you put out, the yacht will bump about in an uncomfortable manner if there is any strength in the wind, and the fenders will probably chafe through.

If there is any tide running you must of course allow for its effect. For example, if wind and tide are both in the same direction you will have to shoot up harder into the wind because the tide will kill the yacht's way. If wind and tide are in opposite directions, and of about equal force, you should stop the vessel a short way from the quay, as the tide will carry her on to it. Remember that you can always control the speed of a yacht when going to windward or reaching by starting the sheets so that the sails are not full. In this way, you can jog along slowly towards your objective.

Situations of this kind are always difficult to appreciate on paper, but when you have tried it out in practice, you will soon get the hang of it all and come to know instinctively how to coax your yacht into and out of all sorts of places. A great friend of mine is a master at this and it always gives me enormous pleasure to sail with him. He has owned his yacht for some 15 years, and he and she know each other's ways. He has a small auxiliary engine, but seldom uses it. Under mainsail and jib and often under jib only, he manoeuvres in and out of crowded anchorages as if he was at the helm of a twin-screwed motor launch. It is not that he has no use for the auxiliary. On the contrary, in calms when time is short, and on many occasions when the catching of a tide means the saving of many hours, the 'mechanical topsail' (an oar is termed a 'wooden topsail') is always brought into play. It is just that he is a natural seaman and on the majority of occasions finds it simpler to manoeuvre his yacht under sail.

There is so much 'rush' in this modern life, that I think it not only delightful but extremely good for one to have to do things slowly; to know that if you are rowing from the boatyard to the yacht against the tide, it is going to take you twenty minutes, however hard you may pull. And if you *must* wait four hours for a fair tide, not to worry, but to enjoy the sun and air, and watch the seagulls, or turn in a splice or read a book.

HULLABALOOBALAY

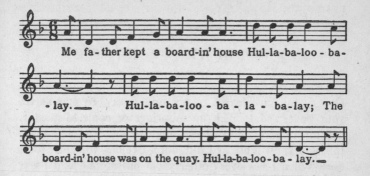

Me fa-ther kept a board-in' house Hul-la-ba-loo-ba- lay. —— Hul-la-ba-loo-ba-la-ba-lay; The board-in' house was on the quay. Hul-la-ba-loo-ba-lay. —

The boarding house was on the quay;
    Chorus.
The lodgers were nearly all at sea.
    Chorus.

A flash young fellow called Shallow Brown,
    Chorus.
Followed me Mother all round the town,
    Chorus.

Me Father said, 'Young man, me boy,'
    Chorus.
To which he quickly made reply,
    Chorus.

Next day when Dad was in the Crown,
    Chorus.
Mother ran off with Shallow Brown.
    Chorus.

Me Father slowly pined away,
    Chorus.
For Mother came back on the following day.
    Chorus.

CHAPTER 13

Helmsmanship, Trim, and Ballast

—

ONCE you have learnt to get under way, to manoeuvre your boat, and to pick up moorings or come to anchor, you must guard against becoming careless. You may think that you know it all, as I did, until, like me, you enter for a race. When I saw every other yacht passing me as if I was standing still, I was at first annoyed and then puzzled. I blamed the boat, the cut of the sails – in fact I laid the blame everywhere but in the right quarter – myself!

The answer can be summed up in one word – helmsmanship. Helmsmanship is an art and must be acquired. The helmsman must develop 'good hands' just like a horseman. Just as a good horseman feels his mount, so does the good helmsman feel his ship. He knows whether or not she is correctly balanced and trimmed, and he can sense at once whether she is going well or labouring under too much canvas or is going sluggishly under too little.

There is one good rule in helmsmanship – let the boat do the sailing. A well-balanced boat can quite often sail herself better than you can sail her. A boat that tries to turn up into the wind is said to carry 'weather' helm; while a boat with the opposite characteristic is said to carry 'lee' helm. If your boat has heavy weather helm, it is an indication that something is wrong. Examine the trim. To understand this question of trim and how to counteract lee or weather helm we must examine for a moment the relationship between the sail plan and the hull. Every hull has a point in the centre of its profile which is known as the centre of lateral resistance. If you attached a rope to the

C.L.R. and pulled sideways, the ship should move bodily without turning. This was actually done in the Royal Navy in the old days, to find the position for a boat's false keel. Similarly, if you balanced a silhouette of the ship on a knife's edge, the point of balance would be the C.L.R. (see Fig. 42).

Now in the sail plan there is a point in the centre called the centre of effort. This centre, which is of course a theoretical centre, is found in the following manner. Let us suppose your boat is a Bermudan sloop. Taking the mainsail first; draw a line from the head of the sail to the centre of the foot, and another from the clew to the centre of the luff. Where they cut gives you the C.E. of the mainsail. Repeat the process with the jib. Now join the two centres (x and y). From x raise a perpendicular, and from y drop a perpendicular. Call the two extremities of these perpendiculars p and q. The proportion of px to yq should be in exact ratio of the proportion of the area of mainsail to the jib, in that order. Join pq, and where pq cuts xy gives you the C.E. of the sail plan. If your boat has two headsails, first find the C.E. of the fore-triangle by the same method and then proceed as above. If she is gaff-rigged divide the mainsail into two triangles and find their combined C.E. By dropping a perpendicular from the C.E. of the sail plan to the L.W.L. you can compare its position relative to the C.L.R. (see Fig. 42).

The C.E. should be in front of the C.L.R. If we had a small mainsail and a very large jib the centre of effort would move forward, and as you expect, the boat's bow would tend to be pushed away from the wind; in other words, she would be carrying lee helm. If, on the other hand, we have a large mainsail and a very small jib, the opposite is the case and our ship would carry weather helm (see Fig. 43).

Following the same line of thought, if we sheet the jib in much harder than the mainsail, the jib will be offering

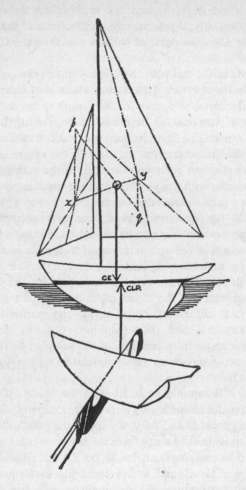

Fig. 42 – How to find the centre of effort of the sails and the centre of lateral resistance of the hull. The relationship between these two determines the balance of the ship.

more resistance to the wind than it should, and you will get lee helm. If the jib is sheeted too slackly and is not doing its fair share of the work, the boat will carry weather helm.

To sum up. Anything that disturbs the relationship between the C.E. and the C.L.R. will be reflected in the helm. Although it would appear that if the C.E. is in front of the C.L.R. you should get *lee* helm, in point of fact you do not. The reason is that as soon as the boat is heeled over the C.E. is outside the C.L.R. and you get a swinging 'moment' towards the wind's direction, thus giving strong weather helm. To reduce this, but leave just a little weather helm, designers put the C.E. in front of the C.L.R., by an amount that can be calculated to meet each case.

So much for theory. Now to translate this theory into practical application. It is fair to assume that if your boat and sails are designed by a competent craftsman the yacht will balance provided you trim your sails correctly, but where you must look out is when you have to reef. As we shall see in Chapter 14, your yacht's mainsail will have some means of being reduced when the force of the wind is too strong, and to match this reduction of the mainsail's area, you will have at least one spare jib, considerably smaller than the working jib.

Now supposing you are sailing with the small jib and reefed mainsail. The wind lightens a bit, so you shake out the reef in the mainsail, but being lazy (forgive me, please, reader) you do not change the small jib for the working jib. Now the C.E. is a long way aft of the C.L.R. and you will find the yacht has a heavy weather helm. Answer? Set the large jib. Similarly, if you have double-reefed your mainsail and are still carrying the large jib, the C.E. will be well forward of the C.L.R., and a lee helm will result. Answer? Set your smallest jib.

In the case of a very heavy weather helm when you have to hold the tiller at quite an angle, by easing the tiller to

Fig. 43

the centre of the boat now and again you will spill the water behind the rudder. This will greatly increase the boat's liveliness and speed.

Timing counts too. Watch the action of the waves and the movement of the boat, and time your movements of the tiller. Eventually, you will do this automatically.

As well as trimming our boat by her sails we must pay careful attention to her ballast. The performance of any boat can be greatly improved by proper ballast. Ballast is of two types; inside and outside. The outside ballast consists of a shaped piece of lead or iron, known as the ballast keel, which is built into the keel of the boat and held in position by a number of very strong bolts. The inside ballast consists of pieces of lead or iron in handy sizes so that one man can lift them. They are stowed inside the boat in such a way that the weight is borne by the timbers and not the planking. Pieces of wood are sometimes fitted between the ballast to prevent it working loose and shifting.

With regard to interior ballast, it is wise to assume that a boat is improperly ballasted. Ballast is generally removed when a yacht is laid up and it is seldom put back in exactly the same way. By moving interior ballast a great deal can be done to improve (or worsen) the ship's performance. If your boat is slow and sluggish, if she seems to be sunk too deep into the water, if it takes a gale of wind to heel her over at all, it is probable that you have too much ballast aboard. If the boat is very tender (heels over very readily) and over-lively, if she appears to want to put her deck under water, if you are forced to reef while other similar craft carry on, then you have not enough ballast.

Ballast should always be stowed as near the ship's fore-and-aft line and as low down in the hull as possible. You will have to decide whether to bunch the ballast up or spread it out to the ends of the boat.

If you bunch it all amidships, the yacht will be lively in response to the helm. She will come about easily, will be easy to steer and not likely to hang in stays. If you spread the ballast out along the length of the keel, the yacht will be steadier on the helm, she will be less likely to pound when punching into a hard sea and she will be more sedate generally. She will cleave through the waves and what spray does come aboard will travel the entire length of her, making a wet ship; whereas the craft with ballast amidships may pound more, but will throw the spray off on either side. All iron ballast should be red-leaded or painted with black varnish as a guard against rust.

A ship with all outside ballast will be more able to 'stand up to her canvas', but she will be more jerky and less comfortable than a vessel with inside ballast. As a rough guide, the usual proportion of ballast to the displacement of the ship is slightly less than half.

Too much importance cannot be laid on this question of trim and ballasting. The performance of your boat is vitally affected by it. To get a yacht ballasted correctly may mean quite a lot of experimental work, but it will be worth it. When you buy your boat, if she has inside ballast, see if the owner has a diagram or can give you some guide as to how it was stowed. This should give you a starting point, and if then she is not quite balanced, bear in mind the remarks in this chapter, and begin to experiment.

MORE ODDS AND ENDS

Always know what the tide is doing.

Many wrecks are caused by bad ground tackle, inadequate anchors and chains.

A dinghy sailor should tuck the tail of his shirt up – it is good to have something dry to pull down over a wet behind.

Arrangements for efficient lighting for chartwork are essential.

Be sure the anchor is shackled to the cable before throwing it over the bows.

Check the accuracy of your compass as often as you can on known bearings, such as two objects in line.

A good start is a race half won.

In bad weather keep a good offing and don't get embayed.

Learn how to morse with a flash lamp; it is very useful and may save your life.

Keep a good log or record. It is easy to forget when cruising.

Remember that a channel that looks easy on a chart is not always so in practice; in bad weather and broken water, buoys are often very difficult to see.

Always carry one more pullover than you think you are going to need.

When approaching a mark ahead, look for it where you don't expect it – it may be there.

When buying a ship, treat with suspicion such remarks as 'she makes just enough water to keep her sweet'.

On the weather side of sandbanks there may be a breaking sea in strong winds.

Remember that the man on a big steamer's bridge cannot see through her bows.

Although you may feel a tough sailor with two days' growth on your chin, you appear in a somewhat different light to people ashore.

Glucose or barley sugar are good preventers of seasickness – especially when you are tired.

If the barometer goes below 29.6 get into shelter if you possibly can with safety.

If an owner says his boat is a wonderful sea boat, he probably means that she has no pretentions to speed or appearance.

Fog signals are very deceptive.

A ship hove-to is, for the purposes of the rules of the road at sea, a ship close-hauled on that particular tack.

It has been said that the three most useless things in a boat are umbrella stands, garden shears, and people who write books on how to sail.

CHAPTER 14

Reefing, and Bad-Weather Tactics

'Watch well your glass and for changes be ready.
Lead, Look-out and Log; Helm steady!'

—

YOU should judge the power of the wind in relation to the size of your yacht. What may be a two-reef breeze for a 3-ton sloop may be a whole sailing breeze for a large yacht. When the wind is before the beam, it will be obvious when it increases, but when it is abaft the beam and is as it were 'with you', then it is harder. You should watch the wind for ten minutes or so before getting under way. If it seems to be increasing it is wisest to prepare for a heavier blow. If it is softening, the delay may save you the trouble of taking in a reef and having to shake it out soon afterwards. It is a common fault to overestimate the strength of an onshore breeze and to underestimate the strength of an offshore breeze. When the wind is blowing off the land the sea appears calm. When the wind is blowing onshore, it disturbs the sea far more. Land breezes are usually puffy, because things like hills and woods and houses trap bits of wind that get held up and then, after a deceptively calm patch, hurl themselves at you and catch you unawares. Sea breezes are steady. So when you reef for a land breeze study the duration of the puffs. If they are strong and frequent, reef. If they have long intervals between them, you can probably get away with it without reefing, by luffing up or starting the sheet just to meet each squall. Always remember that whatever happens, you must keep the boat moving through the water.

One sometimes hears yachtsmen talking of how they were 'caught out'. This is a harmful expression. It conjures up pictures of a dreadful fate that must one day overtake the yachtsman if he ever goes out of sight of land. If you go to sea as you should do – that is, fully prepared – you cannot be caught. You will be able to deal with bad weather in a seamanlike way. No one likes bad weather. It is generally very wetting and uncomfortable. It is difficult to cook, and shifting jibs on a pitching fo'c'sle and getting soaked to the skin can be tiresome, to say the least, but you will, believe me, feel an excitement and a satisfaction at seeing the way your little craft rides easily and buoyantly over the seas, and when you are safely back in harbour you will look with new admiration and affection at the staunch little craft which has looked after you so well. And moreover, no matter how well you can handle your craft under normal conditions, it is when bad weather comes along that there is the real test of your seamanship.

Generally a fresh breeze is soon magnified into a 'gale' round the yacht club fireside. If you listen to the weather forecasts and study the movements of the barometer and observe the sky, and moreover plan your passages with an eye on the possibility of having to shelter, there is no reason why you should ever meet anything in the way of bad weather for which you are unprepared.

Let us assume we are at sea, making a passage, and from the weather forecast and the look of the weather we may expect an increase in the wind's force. We are sailing before the wind, with working jib and whole mainsail. After a while the wind increases, and in order to judge its strength properly, we turn the yacht and bring the wind ahead. After sailing for a moment on a close reach it is clear from the manner in which the yacht is being 'pressed over' more and more by the wind so that she is staggering along with her rail awash that it is time to reef. Now the question arises, one reef or two? (Our yacht has the ordinary point reefing – see Fig. 44.) Once more we study the weather. The glass has dropped more. Shortly we shall have to alter course and sail close-hauled. Yes, we will be well advised to take in two reefs and set the small jib. The secret is to be prepared beforehand. Things have a way of happening very quickly at sea.

It is perfectly possible to reef under way, and if sailing in a long race you would do so. On the other hand, if time for any reason is not important, it is easier, in a small boat, to lower the sails and drift while you tie in the reefs. If there is not sufficient sea-room, you must keep going. If there are two of you aboard, you can lower the mainsail and sail under headsail or headsails. Another common and excellent method is to heave-to (page 168). It is entirely a matter of choice. The first thing to do is to take the weight of the boom off the mainsail, by topping the former up with the topping lift. Just as you tied down the tack cringle in bending the mainsail to the boom, so you tie down the cringle in the luff of the sail at the first reef. You rig an outhaul through the cringle in the leech, pass it over a sheave in the first reef bee block in the outboard end of the boom, haul it hand-tight, and make it fast to a cleat on the boom (see Fig. 44).

If you are reefing under way, you should lower the mainsail so that the cringle on the luff comes down to a position where it can be tied securely to the boom with a reef knot. The cringle in the leech can then be pulled down to the boom at the bee block. Now take the leech between the first reef cringle and the clew. Roll it up tightly and place it on the top of the boom. Then tie down the cringle in the leech to the boom with a line. Notice that there are now two lines holding the cringle in the leech to the boom, the line you have just tied and the outhaul. Next, seize the middle of the part of the sail between the foot and the first reef. Roll it carefully up and tie in the reef points with reef knots. You

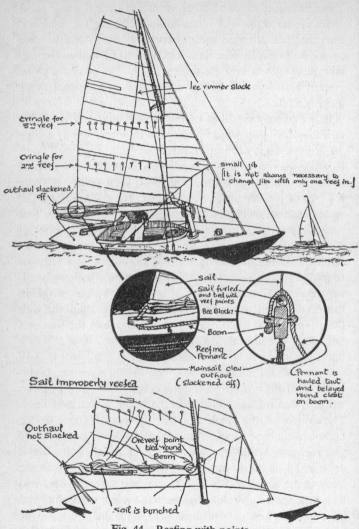

lee runner slack

Cringle for 3rd reef →

Cringle for 2nd reef →

outhaul slackened off

small jib
[It is not always necessary to change jibs with only one reef in.]

Sail

Sail furled and tied with reef points

Bee Blocks

Boom

Reefing Pennant

Mainsail clew outhaul (slackened off)

(Pennant is hauled taut and belayed round cleat on boom.

Sail improperly reefed

Outhaul not slacked

One reef point tied round Boom

sail is bunched

Fig. 44 – Reefing with points.

will have to pass one line of each point under the sail. Do not tie the points round the boom, and be careful not to tie a point in the first reef to a point in the second reef. This is done much more easily than you might imagine. To guard against it, take both ends of the point and pull them alternately. If a pull on one side is not immediately felt on the other, you have two different points. You must smooth out the reefed part of the sail and make it as small as you can. Captain Illingworth in *Offshore* recommends getting the boom actually into the boom crutches before reefing, so as to stop it swaying about with the movement of the ship.

Now we have our first reef tied in. For the second, we repeat the process. This time the leech outhaul will be rove through a second bee block, nearer the mast than the first, and the points will all be tied in on the opposite side of the sail to the first one. As we tied the first reef in on the port side, we must tie the second one in on the starboard side. We must of course use separate lines for the luff and leech cringles and separate outhauls. If you have to tie in a third reef, you must tie it in on the opposite side to the second reef. Furthermore, if you have to tie in two reefs (and certainly if you have to tie in three) you will have to remove the lowest batten from the sail. When tying in reef points it is generally best to start at the luff and work aft. Finally ease off the topping lift.

Now we will assume that we have tied two reefs in the mainsail. The next thing to do is to hand (take down) the jib and set the smaller jib in its place. Some modern yachts are equipped with twin forestays, so that a second headsail may be hanked on and hoisted simultaneously with the lowering of the first. Your boat will probably have a single forestay, though, and it is possible to effect a rapid change of headsails in the following way: Bring the second headsail to the fo'c'sle and, while the first headsail is still hoisted, snap the hanks or spring hooks on to the forestay *underneath* the lowest spring hook of the first jib. (You may have to unsnap the lowest hook of the first jib to give sufficient room on the forestay for all the hooks of the second jib.) When all the hooks are on, unshackle the tack of the first jib, or if the yacht is fitted with a tack downhaul (see Fig. 7) slacken away and then unshackle from the tack. Then shackle on the tack of the second headsail. If there is no tack downhaul, the tack will probably be shackled on to a ring-bolt in the deck or on the stem-head. Now lower away the jib halliard. It is best to take the halliard off the cleat on the mast and bring it for'ard. Then, as you lower away, you can gather in the jib as it comes down. In a small boat, it is best to have only one on the fo'c'sle, but if there are two of you, one should lower away while the other gathers in the jib and at the same time quickly casts off the spring hooks. As soon as the jib is down, unshackle the halliard from the head and shackle it on to the head of the second jib. Meanwhile the second member of the crew unshackles the jib sheets from the clew of the first jib and shackles them on to the clew of the second. If you are single-handed you will do this yourself after the first jib has been lowered and unhooked and the second jib shackled on to the halliard. Now hoist away and belay round the cleat. If a tack downhaul is fitted, set it up, and then, taking the first jib with you, go aft and trim the sheets. Stow the first jib and you are ready to proceed.

When reefing under way it is easiest to sail close-hauled in order that the boom may be as far inboard as possible. Shaking out a reef is done by reversing the process of tying one in. You untie the reef points, beginning at the middle point. When all are untied, cast off the luff hold-down, then the leech hold-down and finally the leech outhaul. If the luff and leech hold-downs are cast off before the reef points you will almost certainly tear the sail. In a gaff-rigged boat, after you have shaken out a reef, lower the peak into a horizontal position before hoisting sail again. Always hoist cautiously after shaking out a reef, in case you have not untied all the points.

Remember to preserve the fore-and-aft balance of the sail plan. If you have double-reefed the mainsail, you will certainly need to change jibs, and if you have three reefs in the mainsail you may have to change again, or if you have no smaller jib, it may be that the vessel will balance

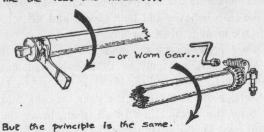

DRUM AND WIRE METHOD....

topping-lift shackles on here.

Wire coiled round drum

Hauling on wire A causes boom to revolve and sail rolls up round it.

This fitting does not revolve with boom.
main sheet shackles on here
If the end of the boom projects well beyond the taffrail, it will be necessary to use a claw-ring for the main sheet
The claw-ring allows the boom to revolve and roll up the sail inside it.

This is the principle of Roller-reefing. There are various ways, as well as the one above, of causing the boom to revolve; like the Pawl and Ratchet....

— or Worm Gear....

But the principle is the same.

Fig. 45 – Roller reefing. A handy method of shortening sail.

better without any jib at all, though this is not to be recommended, as the moment you lower your headsail, the mainsail's efficiency is decreased.

Fig. 45 shows how the mainsail can be reefed by rolling it round the boom. When using this method, after setting up the topping lift, the halliard (or halliards) is eased slowly, and as the sail is lowered, so you roll it round the boom. This method of reefing, provided that the gear is strong enough, is a handy and efficient method of shortening sail, and is met with nowadays aboard all classes of yacht.

Now, to return to our vessel. We have so far tied two reefs in the mainsail and have set the small jib. The yacht will not point as close as before, but as we are running for the moment, this does not affect us. We carry on for a while, but the wind is still increasing; it means to test us this time, by the look of things, and soon it is clear that we must reduce canvas still further. We shall shortly have to alter course, and that will bring the wind on the beam. As the wind is increasing steadily and the glass has fallen still further, we deem it wise to set the trysail and storm jib. The storm jib and trysail are both made of heavy canvas and have heavy bolt ropes and fittings to withstand strong winds. We wait for a smooth (a smooth patch in the waves) and heave-to while we get the trysail's gear ready. To heave-to, pull the jib to windward in line with the mast, haul in the main sheet and lash the helm down about half way. Watch how the ship behaves and trim sheets and tiller to get her to lie in the most comfortable way.

The trysail is a loose-footed sail and has no boom. It may have a small gaff or it may be thimble-headed and look like a Bermudan sail (see Fig. 46). The trysail sheets are double sheets. Now we have all the gear on deck and are ready to bend the trysail. First of all, then, lower the jib to prevent the yacht paying off when the main is off her. Next we must lower the mainsail. First, set up the topping lift. Then lower and furl the mainsail and tie it securely to the boom with the gaskets or tiers. Now lower the topping lift and ease the boom down either into a crutch or, if there is no suitable crutch, to the deck, and lash it

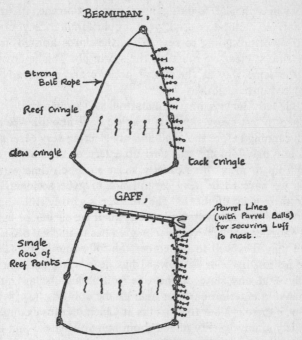

Fig. 46 – Trysails.
Loose-footed. Most Bermudan craft have slides secured to the luff, to run up the ordinary mainsail track.

securely. We cast off the main halliard from the head of the mainsail and shackle it to the head of the trysail. Now the trysail will either have slides on the luff that will run up the ordinary mast track or it will have parrel lines and ash parrel balls (see Fig. 46). After fitting the slides in the track or securing the parrel lines, hoist the trysail. The parrel lines can be secured while you hoist, as each parrel

line comes to the foot of the mast. The trysail sheets are
generally led through stout blocks on each quarter. They
are sometimes in the shape of purchases – a double whip
or luff (see Fig. 50). They hook on the tail of the standing
block in each case, hooking into a ring-bolt on each quarter.
Whatever method is used, you should familiarize yourself
with it before going to sea. When the sail is hoisted, trim
the sheets. Next we must set the storm jib. This is hoisted
in the same way as the No. 2 jib. We are now ready to
proceed once again.

But lady luck is not with us today. The wind is determined to test every shred of gear we have aboard. We are
still running before the wind and are steering very carefully.
As any ugly-looking seas curl up astern of us, we put the
helm up to meet them exactly stern on. Each time we do
this we have to be very careful not to gybe accidentally.
But there is no doubt that the weather is getting still worse,
and we are faced with a decision. Shall we shelter or carry
on? Sooner or later every yachtsman has to make a decision
like this. It is well to remember the following hints: (1) If
the nearest harbour to leeward has deep water and can be
entered at any state of the tide you should be all right.
(2) Avoid entering harbour against the ebb tide. (3) Never
enter if there is a bar to cross (as at Chichester for example).
(4) If you have plenty of sea-room and your vessel and her
gear are sound, you will be perfectly safe riding out the
gale at sea, although it will not be comfortable. Note: For
a description of a yacht riding out gales, *Rough Passage*
by Commander R. D. Graham, *The Southseaman* by James
Weston Martyr, and *Sailing Alone around the World* by
Captain Joshua Slocum all give very good and lifelike
accounts. If you are of nervous disposition or excessively
imaginative don't read these accounts; furthermore don't
go to sea. All seamen must expect to meet bad weather
sooner or later, and while no one likes it, its bark is

generally far worse than its bite. So if you have sea-room and you are doubtful of the harbours under your lee, stay at sea ; you may get scared but you will be safer there than if you tried to run to an unknown haven for shelter.

To return to our problem. We decide to heave-to. This will give us the opportunity to get some hot food and drink, which is very important. Although we may not feel like it, it is worth making a real effort. Even though we do not feel seasick at the moment, hot food will prevent us from becoming so later and will also prevent us from becoming exhausted and low-spirited.

When you have hove-to, reeve a line through the cringle in the clew of the jib and make the two ends fast. The line should not be as taut as the jib sheet itself. Its purpose is to keep the jib secured in case the sheets carry away, which may easily happen in very strong winds. If you have no preventer, as this line is called, and the jib sheets part, the sail will flap about wildly and will be difficult and even dangerous to recapture. Next see that everything on deck is securely lashed. Put extra lines round anything sizeable like the dinghy. Having done these things we can go below and see about that hot food and drink.

If however the wind force increases still further, it will no longer be safe to heave-to. Wind force is generally measured and referred to in weather reports by numbers. This is called the Beaufort Scale. I reproduce it here:

Beaufort number	Description of wind (1)	Specification of Beaufort Scale.		Limits of speed. Nautical miles per hour. (4)
		For coast use, based on observations made at Scilly, Yarmouth, and Holyhead. (2)	For use on land, based on observations made at land stations. (3)	
0	Calm.	Calm.	Calm: smoke rises vertically..	Less than 1
1	Light air.	Fishing smack just has steering way.*	Direction of wind shown by smoke drift, but not by wind vanes	1–3

	(1)	(2)	(3)	(4)
2	Light breeze.	Wind fills the sails of smacks, which then move at about 1 – 2 miles per hour.	Wind felt on face; leaves rustle; ordinary vane moved by wind.	4 – 6
3	Gentle breeze.	Smacks begin to career and travel about 3 – 4 miles per hour.	Leaves and small twigs in constant motion; wind extends light flag.	7 – 10
4	Moderate breeze.	Good working breeze; smacks carry all canvas with good list.	Raises dust and loose paper; small branches are moved.	11 – 16
5	Fresh breeze.	Smacks shorten sail.	Small trees in leaf begin to sway; crested wavelets form on inland waters.	17 – 21
6	Strong breeze.	Smacks have double reef in main sail. Care required when fishing.	Large branches in motion; whistling heard in telegraph wires; umbrellas used with difficulty.	22 – 27
7	Moderate gale†	Smacks remain in harbour, and those at sea lie to.	Whole trees in motion; inconvenience felt when walking against wind.	28 – 33
8	Fresh gale.	All smacks make for harbour if practicable.	Breaks twigs off trees; generally impedes progress.	34 – 40
9	Strong gale.		Slight structural damage occurs (chimney pots and slates removed).	41 – 47
10	Whole gale.		Seldom experienced inland; trees uprooted; considerable structural damage occurs.	48 – 55
11	Storm.		Very rarely experienced; accompanied by widespread damage.	56 – 65
12	Hurricane.	(Yacht crews decide to take up golf.)		Above 65

* The fishing smack in this column may be taken as representing a trawler of average type and trim. For larger or smaller boats and for special circumstances allowances must be made.

† In statistics of gales prepared by the Meteorological Office only winds of force 8 and upwards are included.

It will be noticed that the vessels referred to in column (2) are fishing smacks of larger size than the average yacht of say 7 or 8 tons, yacht measurement. The latter could continue sailing up to about force 8, when they would probably heave-to. Above force 8, it is really unsafe to heave-to, and the yacht would have to lie to a sea anchor or 'a-hull' (lying with no sail set and no sea anchor out). In England the wind rarely blows above force 8 in the summer months. It will easily be seen when it is no longer safe to lie hove-to. As the wind's force increases the seas will get bigger and bigger and the yacht will be thrown about. She will heel to an alarming angle. The crests of the waves will get bigger and more formidable-looking, and more and more water will come aboard. If this happens, the first thing to do is to get the sails off her. Once you have done this, the yacht will probably lie broadside on and will bob about like a cork on the top of the waves. Water will break over the deck and also into the cockpit. No yacht with a very large open cockpit should go where she might have to stand up to weather of this sort. Nowadays many yachts have self-draining cockpits, that empty themselves, an excellent device. Now will be the time to put the sea anchor over the side, but – and here is a substantial but – the sea anchor (shown in Fig. 47) will work properly only under certain conditions. If the yacht is of the modern type with a cut-away bow, she will not ride well to a sea anchor, especially if she has no mizzen mast on which to set a riding sail to keep her head to wind. On the other hand, if she is of the old straight-stemmed type, with a deep forefoot, she will lie to a sea anchor all right without a riding sail. A modern ketch or yawl will ride to a sea anchor perfectly with the mizzen set, and will ride out a storm in surprising comfort, but unless she has some forefoot to get a grip on the water, a sloop or cutter will not ride well with a sea anchor.

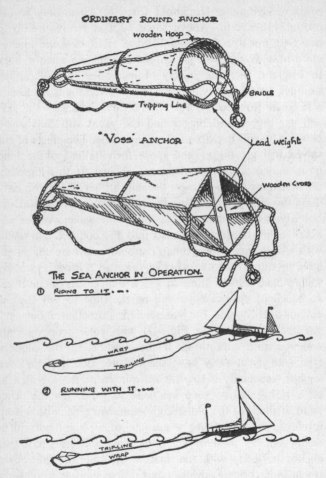

ORDINARY ROUND ANCHOR

Wooden Hoop

BRIDLE

Tripping Line

"VOSS" ANCHOR

Lead weight

Wooden Cross

THE SEA ANCHOR IN OPERATION.

① RIDING TO IT. ⌒⌒

WARP

TRIP-LINE

② RUNNING WITH IT. ⌒⌒⌒

TRIP-LINE

WARP

Fig. 47 – Sea anchors.

However, generalizations are always dangerous and no matter what kind of craft you possess a sea anchor should form part of her equipment. It may easily prove to be of invaluable use one day.

Now how to use it. First get it up on deck (you should keep it below in a handy place) with its tripping line bent on. If you use stout coir rope for the anchor warp you will not need to buoy the sea anchor because coir floats. Now get some hessian or strips of old canvas to take the chafe of the anchor warp in the fairlead. Bend the warp to the anchor, make fast the inboard end of the tripping line, and then stream it over the weather bow. You should pay out enough warp to prevent a sudden jerk coming on it. When the right amount is out, make it securely fast inboard and secure the tripping line, leaving plenty of slack on it. Now wrap the hessian or strips of old canvas round that part of the warp that comes into contact with the fairlead.

If there is time and the yacht is not heeling over too frequently and at too great an angle for safety, it is better to stow the jib, leaving the trysail set. The yacht can then be brought head to wind to stream the sea anchor, and once the latter is over, and the yacht is riding to it, the lowering of the trysail will be a much easier job. If the yacht has close-reefed mainsail instead of trysail it will be necessary to sheet it in hard, set up the topping lift, and lash the boom, before lowering the sail. Put the gaskets on the mainsail as soon as you can. It will chafe if it lies on the deck for long. If your yacht has a bowsprit, to prevent the anchor warp chafing on the bobstay, lash the inboard end of it to the anchor chain and veer the latter for a few fathoms. This is a good idea anyway as it will prevent the warp chafing in the fairlead. The tripping line should be strong. It is held by some that because of the chafing done by the tripping line to whatever it touches, it is better to use a short length of line attached to the sea anchor. When it is desired to get the sea anchor aboard, the boat is hauled up to it by the warp and the tripping line, which, being made of coir, is floating on or near the surface of the water, can be easily retrieved with a boat hook. I cannot claim to have put this into practice, but I include it as a matter of interest. One thing however, is certain, and that is that you cannot get a sea anchor aboard without first capsizing the water out of it by means of a tripping line of some sort.

If your vessel will ride to a sea anchor properly you will be able to endure the gale with safety. If however she will not, and, having taken in all sail, you have been lying 'a-hull', there may come a time when you dare do so no longer, either because too much water is coming aboard or because waves are breaking against the ship's side so violently that you fear they may stave in the hull. In this event you must 'run before it'.

Put a lashing round the lower half of the jib and hoist the head a few feet. The yacht will then pay off very slowly if you assist her with the helm, and will slowly begin to forge ahead, yawing from side to side. The breaking seas will occasionally strike her, but her stern is less vulnerable than her side as she can recoil far more easily.

There is one thing you must always watch out for when running before any form of breaking sea. Never allow the vessel to run too fast. If you do, you will get a big wave breaking over the stern into the cockpit. This obviously can be very dangerous, but the remedy is simple. As long as the vessel is moving ahead more slowly than the waves, they will pass harmlessly underneath her. To slow her down, pay out warps over the stern, to the outboard ends of which you have tied bundles of cushions, old rope, spars, fenders, etc.

You can use the sea anchor also as a means of checking the yacht's speed. The sea anchor should be towed about 5 fathoms (30 feet; 1 fathom=6 feet) astern on both tripping line and warp, the tripping line taking the strain. On the approach of an ugly-looking stern sea, the tripping line is eased quickly and, the warp being taut, the anchor comes into action, holding the yacht back while the wave passes underneath. Once it has passed, the tripping line may be hauled on, the sea anchor capsized and the yacht proceeds as before. This is a useful safety valve when running for shelter and it is desirable to keep the yacht going as fast as is safe, in order to reach a lee or shelter before the storm grows worse.

To end this somewhat sombre section on a good note of pessimism, here is a list of signals a yacht should show when in distress at sea.

EXTRACT FROM THE INTERNATIONAL REGULATIONS FOR PREVENTING COLLISION AT SEA

ANNEX IV

Distress Signals

1. The following signals, used or exhibited either together or separately, indicate distress and need of assistance:

(a) A gun or other explosive signal fired at intervals of about a minute.

(b) A continuous sounding with any fog-signalling apparatus.

(c) Rockets or shells, throwing red stars fired one at a time at short intervals.

(d) A signal made by radiotelegraphy or by any other signalling method consisting of the group ...---... (SOS) in Morse Code.

(e) A signal sent by radiotelephony consisting of the spoken word 'Mayday'.

(f) The International Code Signal of distress indicated by N.C.

(g) A signal consisting of a square flag having above or below it a ball or anything resembling a ball.

(h) Flames on the vessel (as from a burning tar barrel, oil barrel, etc.).

(i) A rocket parachute flare or a hand flare showing a red light.

(j) A smoke signal giving off orange-coloured smoke.

(k) Slowly and repeatedly raising and lowering arms outstretched to each side.

(l) The radiotelegraph alarm signal.

(m) The radiotelephone alarm signal.

(n) Signals transmitted by emergency position-indicating radio beacons.

2. The use or exhibition of any of the foregoing signals except for the purpose of indicating distress and need of assistance and the use of other signals which may be confused with the above signals is prohibited.

3. Attention is drawn to the relevant sections of the International Code of Signals; the Merchant Ship Search and Rescue Manual and the following signals:

(a) A piece of orange-coloured canvas with either a black square or circle or other appropriate symbol (for identification from the air).

(b) A dye marker.

There are some elementary things about weather forecasting which all who go to sea should know. Firstly Nature has provided us with signs that enable us to forecast coming changes with reasonable accuracy – the colour of the sky at sunrise and sunset, and the shape and movement of clouds. By studying the behaviour of sea birds, animals, and fish we can learn a lot about the coming weather. Finally there is the barometer – an instrument no vessel that goes to sea should be without. The barometer is an instrument that records any change in the air pressure.

There are two main types of pressure disturbances to be met with in the waters that surround the British Isles: the anticyclone and the depression. An anticyclone is a system of winds which revolve in a *clockwise* direction about an area of *high pressure*. It brings fair weather. The air is fairly dry and the wind moderate in strength. It is a stable system and liable to last for some time. In the centre of the system there is very often a calm, the surface air is damp and there is a good possibility of a fog. Anticyclones give warning of their passing by a steadily falling barometer and by the clouds changing their shape. A depression is a low pressure system. It is caused by an *anti-clockwise* circulation of air about an area of *low pressure*. Its characteristics are strong winds and rain. This system moves generally in a north-easterly or easterly direction, and, fortunately, travels rapidly. Warning of its approach is given by 'mares' tails' and a falling barometer. Other signs of its approach are a halo round the moon and a steady banking up of low cloud growing denser and denser. The wind shifts in an anti-clockwise direction (backs) and the air becomes close. Finally, the wind increases in force accompanied generally by heavy rain.

The centre of the depression can sometimes be spotted as the system passes over by the barometer ceasing to fall any further. If the centre is passing directly overhead, the wind will suddenly back about 180 degrees, continuing to blow hard and in consequence setting up a nasty sea. If the centre of the depression passes to the southward of you, then the wind will have been moving to your right as you face the centre, but once it has passed, although the wind will continue to back, the barometer will begin to rise. If passing to the northward of you, the barometer will not change very much but will rise slightly as the wind begins to back. The nearer you are to the centre of the depression, the stronger is the force of the wind.

After the centre has passed, the weather will begin to improve. Fine periods will be interspersed with squally winds and showers, and the barometer will rise steadily. If the wind goes to the north-west and remains there, or goes to the north-east, a fine spell is due; if it backs to the southward, and the barometer begins to fall again, then another depression is on the way.

The general sequence of events as described is so consistent that provided you know the shape, course, and speed of the system, you could forecast with great accuracy the changes to be expected. Unfortunately the shape, course, and speed do not remain constant, owing to the presence of land, and make the job of forecasting much harder. Out in the open sea these three factors do remain fairly constant, but we are most likely to be concerned with coastal weather conditions.

As far as the yachtsman himself is concerned, his best course is to get a general idea of the weather by listening to the weather reports on the wireless, and then, by observing local signs, endeavour to form his own forecast for the area in which he will be sailing.

To start with, a rapid movement of the barometer is always the forerunner of unsettled weather. A steady barometer, especially when the surrounding air is dry, means a fine spell. Generally speaking the glass falls for a southerly wind and rises for a northerly wind. A large drop in the barometer means strong winds and rains; if the air is warm the wind will most likely be from the southward; if cold from the northward. If the barometer has been very low for some time, the first rise usually means strong winds; in fact this first rise of the barometer often brings the heaviest northerly gales.

If the barometer is steady and it begins to fall with

increasing dampness of the air, then wind and rain from the south, south-east, or south-west, in fact the beginning of a depression, may be expected. The barometer almost always begins to rise before a gale has finished. If it is steady and the air gets drier and the temperature drops, then northerly winds may be expected and a dry period. Before and during a fine spell, the barometer will remain high and steady.

Generally speaking:

A high barometer means fine weather; a low barometer means bad weather; a steady barometer with dry temperature means a continuance of fine weather; a slowly rising barometer means settled weather; a quickly rising barometer means bad weather; a rising barometer usually means less wind or rain, while a falling one indicates more wind and/or rain; a rapid fall indicates bad weather.

The approach of a depression, bringing rain clouds from the westward, can give us an idea of the wind's force – if the rain precedes the wind, then it will blow hard; if the wind comes first, then it will be neither so strong nor of such long duration.

The prevailing wind in the British Isles is south-west. Sea winds usually bring rain, while land winds are dry. When talking of the force of the wind, the Beaufort scale is used. (See pages 171–2.)

Under normal fine-weather conditions the wind shifts round in the same direction as the sun, and if the reverse occurs and an easterly wind backs to the north or a westerly wind backs through south to the east, then bad weather is in store, since this is a forewarning of a depression coming from the westward.

In addition to the wind's movements, and the movements of the barometer, the shapes of the clouds give a further indication of the weather.

Upper Clouds.

Cirrus=white feathery clouds ('mares' tails'). If they remain steady and isolated, good weather will continue. If they assume a regular formation, gradually covering the whole sky, this means bad weather.

Cirro-stratus=a thin white sheet of cirrus completely covering the sky. If of no definite shape and the weather is fine, it will continue. If however, the formation starts by being cirrus and becomes a regularized formation, bad weather will follow.

A halo round the sun or moon in these conditions also means bad weather.

Cirro-cumulus=a collection of white masses of cirrus formed in groups or lines. This is the 'mackerel' sky of sailors. The cirrus, if isolated, mean fine weather will continue; if they fill the sky and come close together, bad weather can be expected.

Alto-cumulus=a large type of cirro-cumulus, arranging itself in tightly packed lines or waves, and completely covering a large part of the sky.

Alto-stratus=a sheet of grey cloud with a bright patch indicating the sun (or moon).

Lower Clouds.

Strato-cumulus=rolls of heavy dark clouds covering the whole sky with occasional blue patches showing through. Generally seen in winter, it means wind but not rain.

Nimbus=the rain cloud. A dark heavy mass of cloud with no definite shape. If broken up into small clouds it is known as 'Fracto-nimbus'.

Cumulus=thick white woolly clouds with clearly defined, flattish lower edges. A fair-weather formation. If rather oily in appearance, and growing in size towards evening, a change in the weather may be expected.

Cumulo-nimbus=heavy masses of cumulus rising high

with a heavy black base of nimbus. This means thunder and heavy squalls, lightning and rain.

Stratus=a layer of cloud somewhat like a fog, not resting on the ground. If broken up by winds, it is known as Fracto-stratus.

A general rule is that rounded clouds mean dry weather.

A rosy sunset means fine weather.

A pale yellow, green, or copper-coloured sunset means bad weather.

A bright yellow sky means wind.

An orange or pale yellow sky means rain.

A dark red sunset also means rain.

A red sunrise means wind and rain.

A grey morning means fine weather.

A 'low dawn' (when the day breaks on the horizon) means fine weather.

A 'high dawn' (when the daylight first shows above a bank of cloud) means wind.

After fine weather, cirrus or cumulus clouds high up and crossing the sky in a different direction from the lower clouds and existing wind, indicate a change of wind towards the direction from which the high clouds come.

Small dark clouds mean rain. Small light grey moving clouds indicate wind. Hard, oily, clearly defined clouds or a hard dark blue sky foretell wind and sometimes rain as well.

Sea birds remain near the land at the approach of bad weather; porpoises swim to windward and jump out of the water.

The appearance of the sky at sunset and sunrise, the direction of the wind, and the movements of the barometer, used in conjunction with the wireless weather report, should enable anyone to plan a passage at sea with reasonable certainty of the weather he will meet. But always remember the old saw:

'Though the weather is fine and the winds blow fair,
Sudden changes may well come to pass.
So do not let security lull prudent care,
And watch well the range of the glass.'

BLOW THE MAN DOWN.

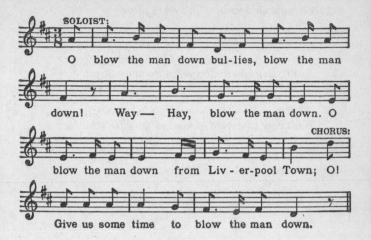

O blow the man down bul-lies, blow the man down! Way — Hay, blow the man down. O blow the man down from Liv - er-pool Town; O! Give us some time to blow the man down.

2. *Come listen to me and I'll sing you a song,*
   Chorus: *Way-Hay, blow the man down.*
   Of the thing that befell me new home from Hong Kong.
   Chorus: *Give us some time to blow the man down.*

3. *As I was strolling down Paradise Street,*
   (Chorus as before).
   A pretty young maiden I chanced for to meet,
   (Chorus as before).

4. *The pretty young maiden she said unto me,*
   There's a fine full-rigged clipper just ready for sea.

5. *So I packed up my sea-chest and signed on that day,*
   And with that sweet maiden I spent all my pay.

6. *The fine full-rigged clipper for Sydney was bound,*
   She was very well-manned and very well-found.

7. *As soon as that clipper was clear of the Bar*
   Her mate knocked me down with the end of a spar.

8. *Her skipper was pacing the break of the poop,*
   And he helped me on with the toe of his boot.

9. *As soon as that clipper had got out to sea,*
   I'd cruel hard treatment of every degree,

10. *So all you young fellows who follow the sea,*
    Give me your attention, just listen to me,

11. *Don't you go a-strolling down Paradise Street,*
    Or just such a chowlah you'll chanc't for to meet.

12. *And I'll give you fair warning, afore we belay,*
    Don't ever take heed of what pretty girls say.

CHAPTER 15

Rigs and Rigging

—

CONSIDERED solely from the point of view of aerodynamic efficiency, the sloop or cutter rig is obviously the best. If windward sailing alone is the criterion, the sloop and the cutter have the advantage. But there are other considerations to be taken into account, suitability of rig to the size of craft, ease of handling, accommodation below decks, and the question of man-power (i.e. the largest sail area one man can deal with properly being 500 square feet, the size of the sails must be dependent on the crew carried).

Let us have a look then at the more common rigs found on yachts today and consider some of their advantages and disadvantages.

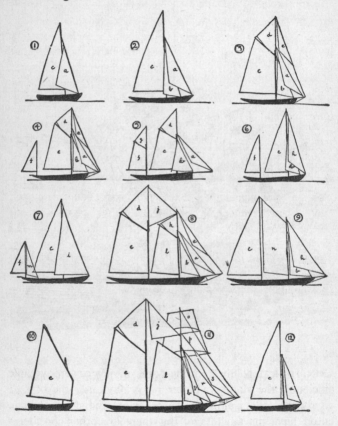

Fig. 48 – Rigs.
The most usual yacht rigs seen today in home waters.
(For references see page 189).

Rigs:

1 Bermudan sloop, 2 Bermudan cutter, 3 Gaff cutter, 4 Gaff yawl (with Bermudan mizzen sail), 5 Gaff ketch (with gaff mizzen sail, trawler type), 6 Bermudan ketch, 7 Bermudan yawl (ocean racing type), 8 Gaff schooner, 9 (Bermudan) Staysail schooner, 10 Balanced lug rig, 11 (Gaff) Topsail schooner, 12 Sliding gunter lug rig.

Sails:

(a) Jib, (b) Staysail, (c) Mainsail, (d) Main topsail, (e) Jib topsail, (f) Mizzen sail, (g) Mizzen topsail, (h) 'Yankee' jib topsail, (i) 'Genoa' jib, (j) Main topmast staysail, (k) Fore topsail, (l) Foresail, (m) Mizzen staysail, (n) Main staysail (takes the place of foresail and main topmast staysail), (o) Fore upper topsail (square), (p) Fore lower topsail (square), (q) Inner jib, (r) Outer jib, (s) Flying jib.

The Sloop (see Fig. 48).

This is the theoretically perfect combination of a large mainsail and a single foresail. It has much to recommend it. The mast, being stepped further forward than in a cutter, enables the cabin to be larger. This is a great point in favour of the sloop rig for small vessels up to 5 or 6 tons. The sloop rig is also easy to handle. The single headsail means only one pair of sheets to worry about. But in larger vessels the sloop rig has its disadvantages. The mast being stepped well forward tends to encourage plunging in steep head-on seas; and it is difficult to heave-to in a sloop.

The Cutter (see Fig. 48).

The cutter is a more effective sea-going rig. The balance of the fore-and-aft triangles makes for efficient windward sailing. In large yachts of over 20 tons, the size of the mainsail can be a bit of a problem, needing a competent crew to handle it, but if kept within reasonable proportions, and if the main boom is not too long, the cutter is one of the handiest and fastest of rigs.

The Yawl (see Fig. 48).

This rig represents an attempt to solve the problem of the large cutter by dividing the area of the triangle into a smaller mainsail and a small mizzen. It is a very popular rig in both large cruising and ocean-racing yachts. It is generally agreed that it is not quite as fast as a cutter, it will not go to windward as well, and in very large yachts requires just as big a crew as a cutter. On the other hand, the mainmast being stepped further forward assists in the accommodation plan, and the mizzen can be used effectively to hold the vessel's head to windward when hoisting the mainsail or when riding out a gale to a sea anchor.

The Ketch (see Fig. 48).

The principal advantage of the ketch rig is that it needs a smaller crew, having a smaller mainsail and a larger mizzen than the yawl. On the other hand, this rig lacks the power of a cutter and is not an efficient rig for windward sailing.

The Schooner (see Fig. 48).

This is a sort of reversed ketch. It is more popular in America than in this country, and is most effective in the larger yachts. It is a poor performer to windward, but makes up a good deal if the wind is on or abaft the beam. It is a very seaworthy rig, because in bad weather the mainsail can be stowed and a trysail set on the mainmast, turning her into a ketch, so that in the worst weather she has her largest sail amidships, where it can be easily handled. Another advantage is that both masts being tied together support each other.

Bermuda or Gaff?

It has been proved by wind-tunnel experiments that the maximum driving power of any sail is developed on its leading edge. The high narrow Bermuda sail plan (see

Fig. 48) which has a larger leading edge than any other, must have more driving power, and is therefore superior to the gaff rig when beating to windward. On the other hand, viewed from a purely cruising standpoint, working to windward in these days of auxiliary power is not the absolute criterion of efficiency. Also, the gaff sail develops more drive than the Bermudan if the wind is anywhere abaft six points on the bow.

The Bermudan sail has no gaff to sag under way and it is easier to lower and hoist. It is also easier to reef and it calls for less man-power in handling.

In general, the Bermudan sail is about 10 per cent more efficient than a gaff sail of the same area, but one must take into consideration the fact that with the former you have a tall mast which can be a big responsibility in a seaway and which must be stayed efficiently if you don't want to lose it in a squall. The fact is that almost all ocean racers have the Bermuda rig and that many offshore passages have been safely made with it. The gaff rig still has its adherents, but for the majority today it is Bermudan every time.

Now as to rigging. This is of two kinds; standing rigging and running rigging. The definitions explain themselves. Standing rigging is rigging that stands throughout the season (except for minor adjustments). Running rigging is rigging that runs through blocks and is continually being hauled on or slackened.

We will take standing rigging first. This is made of flexible steel wire and has great strength. The development of aircraft has led to experiments with wire in order to get the greatest strength with the smallest diameter and lightest weight, and nowadays rigging is not nearly so thick in diameter as it used to be. Uffa Fox, an authority, says that the combined strength of the topmast and main shrouds should equal the displacement of the yacht. Small wire in good condition is far better than heavy wire in poor condition, but all in all, heavy wire will always outlast small wire, and in any case new rigging is cheaper than a new mast. So pay particular attention to your standing rigging.

If the wire passes round the mast or is joined to a rigging screw it will have to be spliced. I should not attempt to do this yourself, to begin with, at any rate. There are several reasons. Firstly, wire is very much more intractable than rope. You can easily get splinters from it, and it behaves, when unlaid, in a most undignified and infuriating manner. Secondly, there are twice as many strands to keep track of; where rope has three or four, wire frequently has seven. If there is no one who will splice wire for you, you can use clamps which will hold the wire pretty well as strongly as a splice.

The wire is held to the deck by means of lanyards or rigging screws. The choice is a matter of taste, although rigging screws are far more commonly used. In the case of lanyards, the wire is spliced round a wooden or lignum vitae block known as a dead-eye. A second dead-eye is shackled to the chain plate. The dead-eyes have holes in them through which the lanyard is passed several times, then round its own part and secured. Rigging screws are of several kinds, but the principle of them all is the same. There are two male screw members with threads running in opposite directions and a female screw member between them, which when turned one way draws the two male members together and moves them away from each other when it is turned the other way. In this way it slackens or tautens up the rigging. Some rigging screws consist of two vertical struts connected to the male members. This is a poor type as it offers no protection to the threads of the male member. Another type met with consists of a long, thin barrel with holes in it through which a tool (like a marline-spike) can be thrust in order to turn it. The best type of rigging screw consists of a barrel that has a nut cast in the middle of it as well as holes so that it can be turned with a wrench or adjustable spanner (a thing, by the way, you should never be without).

There is usually (or should be) some means of preventing the rigging screw from turning back of its own accord when a strain comes on it. The most usual method is by locking nuts at either end. Another method is by cotter pins through both the male members. Otherwise you can use small wire. Locking nuts are the best.

Rigging screws are often of gun-metal or galvanized iron; the latter are generally much cheaper than the former though not so neat-looking. Keep rigging screws, and all metal fittings, well greased. Buy a tin of grease for this purpose.

Chain plates are secured to the hull by bolts. They should be long enough to cover several planks, and, if possible, their fastenings should go through the timbers as well as the planking. They can be outside or inside the planking, but in modern yachts, at all events, are generally placed inside. A yacht looks in some ways smarter if they are inside, but at the same time, outside chain plates give a vessel a businesslike look. There is a certain romance about craft with long bowsprits, fiddled topmasts, and high bulwarks lingering on from the fine old days when sail dominated the seas.

Now let us look at the various shrouds and stays that comprise the standard rigging.

Firstly, the shrouds. The shrouds have one duty – to prevent the mast from breaking and going over the side. They should be set up fairly taut, but not too taut. A good rule is that they should look taut to the eye but not feel quite taut with the hand. A slight play given to the mast, permitting it to bend a little, is a good thing. In the old square-rigged ships the shrouds were never set up too tight, so as to give some degree of elasticity to the masts. Nowadays this elasticity is no longer considered so necessary, but it is still good practice not to set up your shrouds too tight. When the mast bends under sail, the windward shrouds should be very taut and the leeward shrouds should be slack. If the shrouds are set up too taut, the mast will develop a 'S' curve, which is very dangerous. It will try to go through the bottom of the ship, and if it can't do that, it will break. On Bermudan yachts there are generally a pair of main shrouds, leading to a point about half way up, where the spreaders are, and another pair running over the spreaders up to the mast-head. In this case there will be two chain plates each side, one forward of the other. The upper shrouds are always secured to the forward chain plates. Here, the actual sail area is very small, and it is common practice to leave the upper shrouds a little slacker than the main shrouds, so that the mast can bend very slightly. I know of one occasion where some hardy fellows were putting to sea in blustery weather and somebody noticed how slack the topmast shrouds were. 'Oh!' said one, 'That is to save having to reef. Any time it blows too hard the top of the mast bends right over to leeward, and so reduces the sail area.' I do not recommend this method of reefing.

To continue with the forestay. The jib will be hanked on to this, and as the curve which it takes up when the jib is full of wind determines to a certain extent the efficiency of the jib, you will see that it is very important to get the right amount of tension on this stay. A general rule is that when the windward runner is set up and the jib set, the forestay should be taut. When the boat is under way and sailing close-hauled and the jib has wind in it, the forestay will take on a slight curve to leeward. When the mainsail is lowered and the runners are slackened off, the forestay can feel a bit slacker. You will be able to determine by trial and error the best tension for your own particular vessel. If possible get a friend who knows something about it to go out with you and have a look at the rigging.

If you have a fore-topmast stay, it should also feel taut

when the boat is sailing, and slacker when the tension is off
the mast.

Remember that tightening the forestays will make the
mast curve forwards; and, vice versa, if they are too slack,
the runners and the weight of the mainsail (sailing close-
hauled) will make the mast curve aft. Some masts in Bermuda-rigged craft are given a backward rake, but this is a
matter of controversy amongst designers.

Next come the runners. The function of the runners is
really twofold. They support the mast against the forward
pull of the mainsail and headsail when running or on a
broad reach; and when sailing to windward, they help to
keep the forestay (and so the luff of the jib) taut. They
run from two points on the after side of the mast, opposite
the point on the forward side from which the forestay runs.
If the yacht has more than one headsail and the jib is set
on a topmast stay or a jib stay, there will be an equivalent
pair of runners to balance it. Often in this event, the two
runners join half way down on either side of the mainsail, in
a single line. Runners are tautened or slackened by either a
rope purchase or tackle (see running rigging) or by two
metal levers. These levers have the advantage of putting
exactly the same strain on the runner each time. The advantage of a purchase is that the amount of tension on the
runners can be varied at will, e.g. they can be eased off a
little in light airs, so as to slacken the forestay, and give the
jib a little more fullness. Where a purchase is used, a common method in Bermudan craft is to have the eyes in which
the runners terminate working on wire spans running fore
and aft along the side decks. This method puts rather a
heavy strain on the wire spans. Still another method is to
have a metal track fastened to the deck on either side of
the cockpit, along which a slide, shackled to the runner,
can be pulled aft by means of the purchase. When sailing
in a craft with runners, you must keep the weather runner

taut and the lee runner slack, or the latter, even when sailing close-hauled, will be in the way of the mainsail. In racing yachts and most modern cruising yachts there is at least one pair of sheet winches situated one on either side of the cockpit. The fall of the runner purchase can be brought to the winch if the strength of the breeze prevents your getting the proper tension on it. Many Bermudan yachts have a standing backstay from the centre of the after-side of the mast-head down to the centre of the stern. It is set up, like the forestay, by means of a rigging screw. Of course a standing backstay is only possible when the boom stops short of the counter, or if a small bumpkin, projecting out beyond the counter, is fitted. In many modern yachts with a standing backstay and where all sails are set on the fore-topmast stay, runners are dispensed with. If your new boat has this rig, ignore my remarks concerning runners. The absence of runners, when making short tacks, can be a godsend!

So much for the standing rigging. Now let us take a look at the running rigging of a boat. The running rigging of a yacht consists in general of the halliards (mainsail and head-sails), the topping lift, the main sheet and jib sheets. The main and jib halliards are frequently of wire, with a rope purchase (see below) at the fall, while the topping lift and sheets are generally of rope. In very small yachts the running rigging is very simple, but in anything larger than a dinghy, where quite a lot of force is required to haul in the main sheet or to hoist a large sail or a heavy boom, we have to resort to a mechanical device known as a purchase or tackle. A purchase is a length of rope running through one, two, or more blocks so as to increase the power of the person hauling on it. A block consists of an outer shell of wood or metal. In the hollow interior (known as the swallow), a pulley or sheave revolves about a pin. A common block has a rope or wire strop round its outside, fitting into grooves at the top (crown) and the bottom (tail) of the shell (see Fig. 49). An internal bound block has an iron strop inside the shell. The best blocks are made of ash internally bound. These, however, are expensive. Elm blocks with strops round them are much cheaper. There are also good blocks made of stainless steel and plastics, which are excellent. Blocks are measured by their length. The length of a block should be three times the circumference of the rope to enable the rope to run easily. For wire rope the diameter of the sheave should be five times the circumference of the rope.

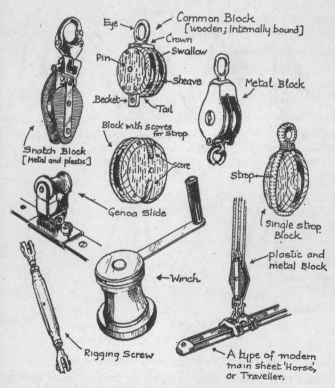

Fig. 49 – Various blocks and deck fittings.

A rope is run through a block for two reasons. Firstly, it changes the direction of the pull. Secondly, it increases the

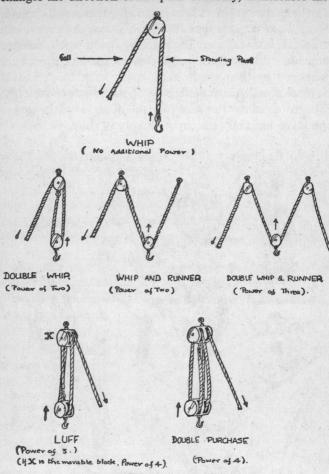

Fig. 50 – Tackles (pronounced 'taicles').

power of the pull. The object of a purchase is to give increased power to the man hauling on the fall. Now take a look at Fig. 50. Here, the single whip gives no additional power because the block is fixed.

The runner however, is a single whip reversed. The single block can move. One end of the line through it is fixed, and the other end is the hauling part. By attaching the hook on the block to whatever is required to be lifted or moved, the power gained is doubled.

In Fig. 50, we see a single whip and runner combined. This is often found in small craft and double power is gained by it.

The double whip consists of a single line rove through two single blocks, the standing part being made fast to the tail of the upper block. The lower block moves. Double power is gained.

A luff tackle gives three or four times the power, depending whether the single or the double block is the one which moves. Thus if the double block moves we get twice the power of a runner, i.e. four times.

And so on. The diagrams in Fig. 50 are self-explanatory. The principle of the whole thing is that where a block is used singly and does not move, like a simple main halliard, no power is gained. As soon as a moving block is fitted, power increases in direct proportion to the number of moving blocks, or the number of sheaves in those blocks (as in the case of a luff tackle).

Now let us see where and how purchases are used in the running rigging of a ship.

Firstly the main sheet. Main sheets are generally of two kinds – double-ended and single-ended. With a double-ended main sheet, both ends of the sheet lead to the cockpit. With a single-ended sheet, one end is secured to the boom or to the deck and the other leads to the cockpit. The advantage of the former is that it can be trimmed or let fly on either side of the cockpit, which can be very handy on occasions. The advantage of the latter is its simplicity.

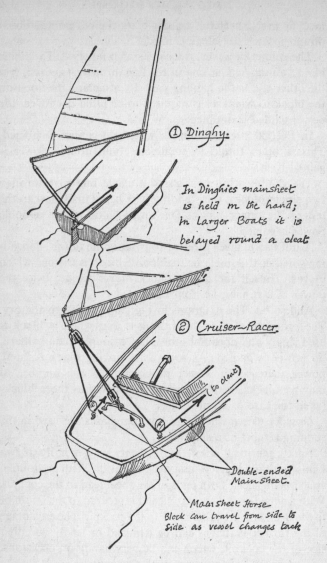

① Dinghy.

In Dinghies mainsheet
is held in the hand;
In Larger Boats it is
belayed round a cleat

② Cruiser~Racer

(to cleat)

Double-ended
Main Sheet.

Main Sheet Horse
Block can travel from side to
side as vessel changes tack

Fig. 51 – Two types of main sheet arrangement.

The main sheet will usually have one of its blocks travelling on a horse (see Fig. 51). This enables you to trim the boom right down to a point beneath it on deck. You can trim it flatter in consequence, and in the case of a gaff sail it prevents the gaff sagging off to leeward, which it would otherwise do.

The block or blocks on the boom, in the case of modern craft which have the end of the boom inboard, are attached to the end of the boom itself or frequently to wire spans, depending on whether the yacht has roller or point reefing. Spans allow the blocks to slide forward when the yacht is running with the boom broad-off and they also distribute the strain along the boom more evenly. In the case of an older type of craft with an outboard boom a claw ring is used (see Fig. 45). If the yacht has an outboard rudder, the horse will have to run over the top of the tiller. According to the size of your mainsail you will need more power to trim it. A mainsail of 500 to 600 square feet can be trimmed easily and quickly with a four-part purchase.

Let us now take a small yacht of about 5 tons Thames measurement and see what her running rigging might consist of. The main halliard in a small yacht will often just be a single whip (see Figure 50). In larger craft with heavier sails a double whip can be used. This should not be necessary in a 5-tonner.

Next the jib halliard. In a 5-tonner this will probably be a single whip, giving no increased power. If the yacht is cutter-rigged, and has two headsails, the staysail will be single-part, but the jib will probably have a block on the head of the sail through which the halliard passes, the standing part of the latter being secured to the mast. This is a good arrangement and gives a power of 2 (a runner). The main sheet can be rigged in a variety of ways. A good double-ended method is to have a double block on the boom with a single block running on a horse and two single blocks on deck, through which are led the two running parts. The jib sheets will be single-part and the topping lift also – a 5-tonner's boom is not too heavy to lift with a single whip.

While we are on this subject, have as many of your blocks as you can of the same size. You can then use the same size rope for many purposes. In a 5-tonner, 1½-inch rope (rope is measured by the circumference) will suffice for everything. The best type of rope – nylon, or manila, or cotton line – is undoubtedly expensive. Nylon has the advantage of remaining really pliable when wet. Italian hemp is very strong and supple. It is extremely expensive. Sisal is cheaper but less reliable. Coir (grass) rope is useful because it floats in water (always throw a grass line to a man overboard). It makes an excellent warp for the kedge anchor as it is resistant to sea water. More and more people use synthetic fibre ropes nowadays. Nylon is the best where both stretch and strength are wanted, but Terylene is better if stretch is *not* wanted. For really tough use Courlene is excellent, while for buoyancy and lightness the best is Ulstron. These new fibres, derived from oil or coal and oil bases, have revolutionized the world of cordage. Synthetic rope is rot-proof and has great resistance to the weather. Another innovation is the use of plaited construction in the making of rope, by using a certain 'core' covered with an outer skin of plaited yarns. Plaited nylon is being used more and more these days.

Lastly, if your sails have a habit of sticking aloft for any reason (and it is not an uncommon occurrence, particularly with the slides and tracks of Bermudan mainsails), rig downhauls. A downhaul is a line reeved from the head or throat of the sail to the deck. Remember some rope shrinks. Do not trim such lines taut when squaring up the boat before going ashore or in the evening. It looks smart, but rain or even dew will be enough to stretch your lines badly. If they are too taut they may do damage. A shrinking halliard that is in reasonably new condition has tremendous power! Synthetic fibre rope does not shrink.

When your running rigging begins to chafe, turn it end for end so that the wear comes on a new part of the line. By turning your lines each season, or more often if it would seem to be necessary, you can make them last you for three or four seasons in normal conditions. You can easily tell if a rope is in good condition by twisting it against the lay and looking at the inside strands. No matter how dirty the outside, if these are in good order and unbroken, the rope is good.

In this revised edition of this book, I can use this space to say a word or two about multi-hull craft – catamarans (two hulls) and tri-marans (three hulls). Rigged usually with Bermudan mainsail and headsail, these fast craft are gaining in popularity both in the racing world and the cruising world. A catamaran is not really the best type of boat for a man who wants to learn to sail (although there is nothing 'difficult' about them). They are specialist craft with certain advantages and certain disadvantages. I have discussed them fully and given three examples in my companion book *Cruising: Sail and Power*. But for the beginner I recommend a small 'single-huller'.

A-ROVING

SOLOIST:

In Am-ster-dam there lived a maid. Mark well what I do say. In Am-ster-dam there lived a maid, And she was mis-tress of her trade. I'll go no more a - rov - ing with you fair maid.

CHORUS:

A - rov - ing, a - rov - ing, since rov-ing's been my ru - in, I'll go no more a - rov - ing with you fair maid.

2. *Her lips were red, her eyes were brown,*
   Mark well what I do say.
   Her lips were red, her eyes were brown,
   And her hair was black and it hung right down,
   I'll go no more a-roving with thee, fair maid.
   Chorus.

3. *I put my arm around her waist,*
   Mark well what I do say,
   I put my arm around her waist,
   Cried she, ' Young man, you're in great haste.'
   I'll go no more a-roving with thee, fair maid.
   Chorus.

4. *I took that maid upon my knee,*
   Mark well what I do say.
   I took that maid upon my knee,
   Cried she, 'Young man, you're much too free,'
   I'll go no more a-roving with thee, fair maid.
   Chorus.

5. *I kissed that maid and stole away,*
   Mark well what I do say.
   I kissed that maid and stole away,
   She wept – 'Young man, why don't you stay';
   I'll go no more a-roving with thee, fair maid.
   Chorus.

CHAPTER 16

Simple Navigation and Pilotage and the Rule of the Road at Sea

—

IN the *Admiralty Navigation Manual*, Vol. I, Navigation is defined as 'the science which enables a ship to be conducted from one place to another in safety, her position to be determined by observations of terrestrial or celestial objects, or by other methods.' It defines Pilotage as 'the conduct of a ship in the neighbourhood of danger, such as rocks, shoals, and narrow waters.' The theory and practice of navigation and pilotage are dealt with in the companion volume to this book. Space is restricted here and I have tried to boil things down to the bare essentials necessary to enable a yachtsman to take his vessel from A to B without going too far off-shore. To navigate a ship properly in all weathers and conditions and for any distance demands quite a fair amount of knowledge, but it is possible to make one's way from place to place in safety with only a knowledge of the rudiments, and although there must inevitably be many things missing in this chapter, yet it should suffice until the reader has the opportunity to go into the subject rather more thoroughly in the companion volume to this book, or elsewhere.

The golden rule in navigation is 'Always know the ship's position'. To do this three things are essential, a compass, a chart of the area in which you are sailing, and a set of navigational instruments – a pair of parallel rules, dividers, and a sharp pencil. These are the basic requirements which you cannot do without. In addition, you should carry a lead line (see Fig. 37) and a patent log for recording the distance the ship has run. There are other useful instruments, such as a hand-bearing compass, a station pointer, a course-setting protractor, etc., but they are not essential. There are also electronic instruments for recording speed, distance, depth, windspeed, etc. Such useful things, beloved of off-shore racers, are very costly.

Let us take a look at the three main requirements. Firstly the compass. The bigger the compass, the more accurate. The principle of an ordinary magnetic ship's compass is simple. It consists of one or more needles so pivoted that they swing and point to magnetic north. Attached to the needles is a compass card marked with points. The card swings inside a receptacle known as the bowl. On the inside of the bowl are four vertical lines known as lubber-lines. The compass should be in such a position in the boat that one

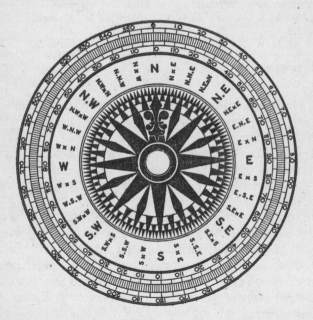

of these lubber-lines points along the ship's fore-and-aft line.

The circumference of the compass card is marked in degrees, of which 0° and 360° are North. Many compasses also have a notation from 0° (North or South) to 90° (East or West) in four quadrants of 90° each. It is also marked into 32 divisions called points. The principal points are North, East, South, and West. These are called the cardinal points. The points midway between them, i.e. North-East, South-East, South-West, and North-West, are known as inter-cardinals. The spaces between the inter-cardinals are further subdivided and then subdivided again. This is called boxing the compass. The points are abbreviated as follows:

3rd Quarter	4th Quarter	1st Quarter	2nd Quarter
S	W	N	E
S by W	W by N	N by E	E by S
SSW	WNW	NNE	ESE
SW by S	NW by W	NE by N	SE by E
SW	NW	NE	SE
SW by W	NW by N	NE by E	SE by S
WSW	NNW	ENE	SSE
W by S	N by W	E by N	S by E
W	N	E	S

The points notation is still used largely in yachts, fishing vessels, and sailing ships where steering is by the wind, and it is thus seldom possible to steer 'to a degree'.

It will be seen that there are therefore three different ways of saying North-East, i.e., North-East, N45°E, and 045° (the 0° – 359° notation is given in *three* figures always to avoid confusion).

In the navigational examples in this chapter I have employed the 0° to 359° notation as this is commonly used nowadays and is very easy to understand. But in any case for those who prefer to think in terms of points the conversion may be rapidly made. And here to help you are the three ways of graduating a compass card, shown in tabular form:

Points	Quadrantal	Three figure
N	N	000°
NNE	N22½°E	022½°
NE	N45°E	045°
ENE	N67½°E	067½°
E	E	090°
ESE	S67½°E	112½°
SE	S45°E	134°
SSE	S22½°E	157½°
S	S	180°
SSW	S22½°W	202½°
SW	S45°W	225°
WSW	S67½°W	247½°
W	W	270°
WNW	N67½°W	292½°
NW	N45°W	315°
NNW	N22½°W	337½°

In this connexion it is interesting to note that before the days of the magnetic compass the Vikings, who were probably the greatest seafaring race of all time, used to box the compass by taking the direction of the four prevalent winds. These were North-East and South-East (Landnyrdingur and Landsynningur), and South-West and North-West (Utsynningur and Utnyrdingur). Thus they started boxing the compass at NE, using cardinals and inter-cardinals as we do, but with NE, SE, SW, and NW as their cardinal points instead of N, S, E, and W. Even today there are some northern fishing skippers who still use the old Viking compass.

To steer a boat by compass you merely manoeuvre so that the point on the compass-card to which you want to sail comes in line with the lubber-line that points forward.

Now if you take a reading of your ship's course and it is NW, you cannot draw a line on the chart going NW and say 'That is my course'. There are two things to be taken into consideration. Firstly, as you know, the north-seeking ends of compass needles point to magnetic north. Magnetic north does not remain in exactly the same position year after year. On the chart, you will find that there are one or more 'compass roses' dotted about. On a modern (from 1972 onwards) Admiralty chart, the 'rose' shows true bearings, from 0° to 359°. On some other charts, like the Stanford charts, the 'rose' shown is the magnetic, also from 0° to 359°. The north line on a true rose points to 'true' North. The north line on a magnetic rose points to magnetic north, which is located in the northern part of Canada. (In fact it has been known for explorers to find, on passing the magnetic pole, that their compass needles began pointing south!) There are still plenty of the pre-1972 Admiralty charts about, which show both the magnetic rose and the true rose, graduated from 0° – 359°. On very old charts the magnetic ring on the compass rose had the quadrantal rotation.

The difference between the true north and magnetic north is called the 'Variation' of the compass. It is different in different parts of the earth and changes as the relative positions of the two 'norths' change, and moreover it changes yearly because of the actual moving about of the magnetic pole. This movement is predictable, and all charts show on the compass rose the variation at the time when the chart was printed, and the yearly correction which is to be applied, if the chart is not new, to bring the variation up to date. Since this change in variation is very slight it is unnecessary for the navigator of a small yacht to take it into consideration if the chart he is using is only a few years old. Now we have seen that a magnetic bearing will, *if the chart you are using is an old one*, have to be corrected for variation. There is another, and in some ways more important, factor to be considered.

A compass which may point directly to magnetic north when it is bought, may cease to do so as soon as it is fixed in position in the cockpit of your boat. The reason is that the compass needles are very much affected by magnetic

influences in the vessel herself. Ballast, metal fittings, the
engine, water tanks, etc., all affect the compass and cause
it to have what is known as 'deviation'. In large yachts,
these magnetic influences can to a great extent be counter-
acted by the installation of small magnets. This job should
be done by a qualified compass adjuster. He comes aboard,
and sails the yacht on a number of known bearings and by
the insertion of these magnets he corrects the errors in the
compass due to deviation. In a small yacht with a small
compass you will not be able to do this, and even in the
cases where it has been done, the errors are not always completely removed. It is *very important*, however, that whatever
errors of deviation there may be *are known* so that the
navigator may allow for them. To find these errors you must
prepare a 'deviation table'.

This is not at all difficult to do. From a reasonably sheltered anchorage, choose a landmark about 3 miles off. Plot
on the chart the exact position of the ship (three cross-
bearings will do that for you. See the latter part of this
chapter). Now from the chart find the exact magnetic
bearing *from the ship* of this landmark. Then slowly turn
the ship round with the engine (or get a friend to tow her
round with the dinghy), steadying her for a minute on each
of the cardinal and inter-cardinal points in turn. Each time,
note from the compass the bearing of the landmark; write
it down, and alongside it put the precise direction of the
ship's head when the bearing was taken. You will get a
table looking something like this:

Yacht 'Saracen'	Deviation Table	27 May 1965	
Ship's head by compass	Compass bearing of landmark	Magnetic bearing of landmark (from the chart)	Deviation
North	199°	200°	1°E
NNE	198°	,,	2°E
NE	196°	..	4°E

ENE	197°	,,	3°E
East	198°	,,	2°E
ESE	199°	,,	1°E
SE	200°	,,	Nil
SSE	201°	,,	1°W
South	203°	,,	3°W
SSW	204°	,,	4°W
SW	205°	,,	5°W
WSW	204°	,,	4°W
West	202°	,,	2°W
WNW	201°	,,	1°W
NW	200°	,,	Nil
NNW	199°	,,	1°E

Let us assume here that we are using a chart showing an up-to-date magnetic rose. This will have up-to-date variation, and so we are concerned only with deviation, which we can find for whichever course we are steering simply by consulting the deviation table. This deviation can be applied according to a rule of thumb. We have no space here to go into the theory, just learn the rule. It is this: with *easterly* deviation the compass needle is deflected clockwise. Therefore to turn a magnetic course (a course taken from the magnetic rose on the chart) into a compass course (the course to steer by the yacht's compass) apply easterly deviation counter-clockwise. With westerly deviation the compass needle is deflected in a counter-clockwise direction. Therefore, to turn a magnetic course into a compass course apply westerly deviation clockwise. Conversely, to turn a compass course to a magnetic course (that can be plotted on the chart from the magnetic rose), apply easterly deviation clockwise and westerly counter-clockwise.

The same rule applies for variation, but here, in order to simplify things, we are taking all our bearings from the magnetic rose of a reasonably up-to-date chart and variation in consequence does not come into it.

For example. Supposing that our course according to the

chart is north; this is our magnetic course. From a given deviation table we see that when the ship's head is pointing N the deviation is 5°W. Right. Apply the rule 'Magnetic to compass, westerly clockwise', and the course that we must steer is 005°. Conversely, if we are steering north by compass, and we wish to plot this on the chart, we reverse the rule and apply westerly deviation anti-clockwise, giving us a magnetic course to plot on the chart of 355°. It is really very simple!

Next, charts. When things are reduced to essentials, practically all the information required for navigation in a given area is to be found on the face of the chart itself. The only other essential piece of information necessary is the time of high water, which is found from the tide tables or nautical almanack. On a large-scale chart there is shown where it is possible or prudent to go, the best way to go there, the magnetic compass course, the scale, the depths of water, the time when the tide changes and its average rate at neaps or springs, and, frequently, coastal sketches of the skyline and other features like beacons, and even anchorages, and the bearings for approaching anchorages as well as the nature of the bottom. With the imminent change to metrication, depths will eventually be shown in metres instead of fathoms (6 feet) as at present.

Charts are in general of three main types: (a) Passage charts, which show both ends of the contemplated voyage, (b) Coastal charts, which are on a larger scale and in consequence show the dangers more clearly, and (c) Harbour plans. The Admiralty charts, which are, generally speaking, in these three forms, are excellent and are fairly easy to obtain. In addition there are several other different types of chart. While Admiralty charts maintain a degree of excellence which is to be expected, they are on the large side for a small yacht, and some people therefore prefer the folding type of chart like the Stanford charts. These latter usually cover large sections of the coast and have on them a number of harbour plans and detailed tidal information. Charts are expensive if you have to buy many. You should use the most up-to-date charts that you can afford.

A very good tip before making a passage is to study carefully the relevant charts, making yourself thoroughly familiar with them, noticing the nature and height of the coastline and shore marks. By this means you will gain confidence, and will feel almost as much at home entering an entirely new and strange harbour as when you are entering one with which you are thoroughly familiar.

In addition to a selection of charts, you will need a nautical almanack in which you will, amongst other useful information, be able to find the time of high water at Dover. I say Dover because round the British Isles tidal information in the tidal atlases and on the charts is based on high water at Dover. *Reed's Nautical Almanac*, edited by Captain O. M. Watts, is an excellent and most useful book. You will also find a 'pilot' a most valuable book. There are pilots for each main coastal area: North Sea Pilot, Channel Pilot Part I (English coast) and Channel Pilot Part II (French coast), etc. 'Pilots' are produced by the Admiralty and are easily obtainable, like Admiralty charts, from most yacht chandlers or from chart agents.

Now, let us use the navigational instruments to find our course. We will assume you are taking your departure from a point A on the chart, just outside the harbour mouth of your home port. Your intention is to sail to a point B just outside the entrance to another port five miles along the coast. The wind is fair and it is a direct course. Take the parallel rulers and lay one edge on the chart along the direct line between A and B. Parallel rulers can be bought at any yacht chandler. They consist of two rulers fastened together with two arms of equal length so that the rulers may be pulled apart or pushed together and yet their outer edges always remain parallel. A good make of parallel ruler is Luard's. Walk the rulers across the chart from line AB to the nearest compass rose, until the edge passes through the centre of the rose. Notice where the edge cuts the circumference of the *magnetic* rose and read off the direction in points or degrees. This will give you the magnetic course. Then, as you have already learnt, apply the necessary deviation, and that will give you your compass course.

Now there are two factors that we must take into consideration. One is the allowance for leeway and the other is the set of the tide. An easy way to determine your leeway is to sail the compass course for a short distance and then look back at your wake. Estimate the angle which the wake makes with the yacht's course, and this will show you how much you should allow for leeway. If your leeway shows you are being set half a point down to leeward, you will have to steer half a point to windward to compensate for it. Of course leeway differs in each case according to the boat's draft, hull form, etc., and it increases in heavy and especially in short seas. Shallow-draught boats make the most leeway.

The amount of leeway your own yacht makes can only be judged accurately by experience. The first time it blows hard the leeway is sure to be greater than you have previously experienced. A good normal type of cruising yacht only makes appreciable leeway when close-hauled, and in good weather does not make very much then. If there is much sea running, you will find it very difficult to judge the angle of the wake owing to the broken water. An accurate leeway allowance is, in point of fact, a matter of knowing your own particular craft.

We now have a new compass course which has been corrected for leeway, but we still have to reckon with the tide. If a tide allowance has to be made a new *magnetic* course has to be found before deviation can be applied, and it is found in the following way. If the current is fair, that is, running in the same direction as you are sailing, it will

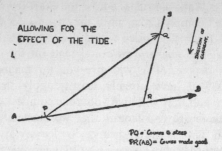

ALLOWING FOR THE
EFFECT OF THE TIDE.

PQ = Course to steer
PR(AB) = Course made good

Fig. 52

merely get you from A to B more quickly. If it is foul, that is, running dead against you, it will merely slow you down without making any difference to your course. But if the current is a cross-current at an angle to your bow or stern or straight on the beam, you must allow for it.

You are sailing, we will suppose, from A to B (see Fig. 52). At any point on the *magnetic* course take a point R and draw a line RS representing the current. The arrowhead shows the *direction* of the current and it will be noticed that the line RS is drawn *opposite* to that direction. Now you must find your yacht's speed through the water from the patent log or, if you have not got one, you must estimate it. Let us say four knots (four nautical miles per hour). Now take your dividers, and place the points along the *latitude* scale (vertical edge) of the chart. The minutes of latitude on the side of the chart each represent one sea mile of approximately 6,080 ft, but as the chart is a flat projection of part of the spherical surface of the earth, the minutes get larger as the poles are approached from the equator. Consequently, when measuring the latitude scale, the middle of the dividers should come over the latitude of the mid-point in the magnetic course laid off, thus averaging out the difference.

Next we look at the tidal information on the chart (or in the tidal atlas). From our Nautical Almanack we have found the time of High Water Dover today, and it is now two hours after that. From the tidal atlas, or from the tidal information on the chart itself, we have found the direction and rate (not speed) of the current. The direction we have already drawn on the chart. The rate is two knots. We measure off two nautical miles from the latitude scale with the dividers and lay it off along RS in the direction of S. We will call the point where the dividers cut RS, Q. With centre Q, and radius 4 miles, cut AB at P. Join PQ with the parallel rulers, carrying PQ over to the magnetic rose on the chart, and read off the new magnetic course. Apply the necessary deviation for the new course and the final result will be the course you must steer.

If you sail in the direction PQ, the current will be driving you in the direction SR so that actually you will 'crab' along the line AB with your nose pointing along PQ, and at any given moment of your passage you will be somewhere along the line AB.

Earlier in this chapter, I mentioned taking your estimated speed from the patent log. This is a very useful instrument (Walker's Excelsior is a good make for small yachts). It consists of an instrument rather like a speedometer, except that it registers, not speed, but distance run through the water. It is worked by a rotator with fins that is towed some seventy-five feet astern of the yacht; a more sophisticated method is an electronic distance run and speed indicator worked by a submerged impeller.

Since the log only gives you the distance travelled through the water, and as the water itself may be moving owing to the effect of the tides, there will be a difference between the distance run through the water as shown by the log and the actual distance made good over the ground. If the tide is fair, you must add to the reading of the log the distance you will have been carried by the tide. If the tide is foul you must subtract that distance. If the tide is across your course,

you must refer to the diagram (Fig. 52). Here you will see
at once that PQ is the course (and distance for a given time)
through the water and PR the course (and distance for the
same time) *made good over the ground.*

On the chart, the plotted course made good is called the
Dead Reckoning. In other words, you know the position
on the chart from where you set out. You know, by the
various calculations we have been discussing, the actual
course you have been sailing, and from the log you know
how far you have travelled through the water. When this
distance has been corrected by an allowance for the tide as we
have described, you can mark the chart with a dot and a small
triangle round it, and that is your dead reckoning position.

Because it is not an absolutely accurate position you put
a triangle round it, as you would round any estimated
position (E.P.). If you know the exact position, that is
called a 'fix', and is always shown by making a small
circle round the dot. Now how do we get a fix? Well, the
easiest method is by taking bearings of fixed objects on the
shore that are marked on the chart. Taking a bearing in a
small yacht is not always easy. Many compasses are in-
conveniently placed. If yours is in a difficult position, buy a
hand-bearing compass and use that (but check it first with
your steering compass). Another easy method of taking
bearings, though not absolutely accurate, is to head the
yacht towards the object it is desired to take a bearing of,
and read off the course on the compass.

The normal way to take a bearing of an object is to look
along the top of the compass at it. If an imaginary line
from your eye, passing through the centre of the compass
and running straight to the object, cuts the compass card
at SW, then the compass bearing of that object is SW. If,
of course, the compass has any deviation for the particular
course you are steering, *that* must be applied according to our
rule of thumb before you can plot the bearing on the chart.

One bearing by itself, however, will not fix the position of the ship on the chart. All it tells you is that at the precise moment that the bearing was taken, the yacht was somewhere along a line running from the object at a given angle. To 'fix' the ship, you must get another line to cross the first. These two 'cross bearings', as they are called, give a definite position. When taking cross bearings the angle between the chosen objects should not be less than about 20 degrees, and the wider this angle can be, the more reliable will be the fix. It is best to take three bearings if you can as the third provides a check on the others. Very likely, when you plot your three bearings on the chart, they will not all three intersect at the same point, but will make a small triangle called a 'cocked hat'. Always choose the point nearest to rocks or land, or anything that constitutes a danger, as your fix.

There are two other methods of fixing the ship that it will be useful for you to know: the 'four-point bearing', and 'doubling the angle on the bow'. These two methods are particularly useful inasmuch as they can be used when only one shore object is available. To take a four-point bearing, note the time or the reading of the patent log when the selected object is 4 points (45 degrees) on the bow, and continue on a steady course until it is abeam and again note the time or the log reading. The interval of time compared with the yacht's speed, or the difference between the log

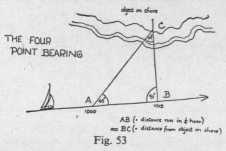

THE FOUR
POINT BEARING

AB (= distance run in ½ hour)
= BC (= distance from object on shore)

Fig. 53

readings, will give the distance you have sailed between the two bearings; and that distance equals the distance from the object when that object is on the beam (Fig. 53 shows how it appears on the chart).

With the doubled angle method, you take a bearing of a given object say 30 degrees on the bow (i.e. if your course is north the object will bear 330°). Carry on a steady course until this bow angle is 60 degrees on the bow (300°). As with the four-point bearing, you note the time or log reading of both bearings and the distance run between the two will be the same as the distance from the object on shore when the latter bears 300° (see Fig. 54).

There is one warning that must be given in connexion with these two methods. In each case the 'course' with which the two bearings make an angle is the *course made good* and not necessarily the *course steered*. When you are working out what bearing a certain angle on the bow will be, it is necessary to work from the *course made good*. That is to say if your course to make good is north and the tide is running to the east, your course to steer will be somewhere to the west of north and not north. As, however, you will be making good north, although your bows are pointing west of north, north is the course which you use to work out the bow angles; and furthermore the distance factor must be determined from the *speed made good* – the speed over the ground and not the speed through the water.

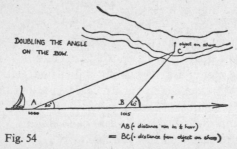

Fig. 54

Making a Landfall

There are few things more exciting than making a landfall
at the end of a passage, and if the destination happens to
turn up exactly where the navigator intended it should, his
satisfaction is enormous. Of course in practice to find
the harbour of one's destination appear dead ahead at the
right moment is a more infrequent than frequent occurrence, because between A and B many variable and indefinite
factors come into play. Tidal variations not shown on the
chart, swell, surface drift and currents, leeway, steering
errors, fog, little inaccuracies of the patent log, deviation
errors: most, if not all, of these factors come into play
on a long passage and make the navigator's task a difficult
one. There are ways and means of nullifying them to a
certain extent and these are discussed at some length in
the volume on Cruising. Here we are dealing more with a
simple coastal passage, and assuming that we have reached
our destination, there are one or two things it is imperative
that we should know. Firstly, an anchorage or harbour may
often have rocks, sandbanks, and other obstructions dotted
round its approaches. In such cases, it is often easy to enter
by sailing in on two or more 'leading marks'. Leading marks
are simply two prominent landmarks easily seen from
seaward which, when brought into line, give a direct
and safe entry into the harbour. Leading marks are generally
marked on a large-scale chart, but even if they are not,
you can make your own by studying the chart, and choosing two easily identified objects, which by bringing into line
will give you a safe bearing on which to enter.

Leading marks are very useful aids to navigation, and
frequently by careful study of the chart several of them can
be found which can be used to show the limit in one or
another direction in which a yacht can stand to windward
when beating up a narrow channel.

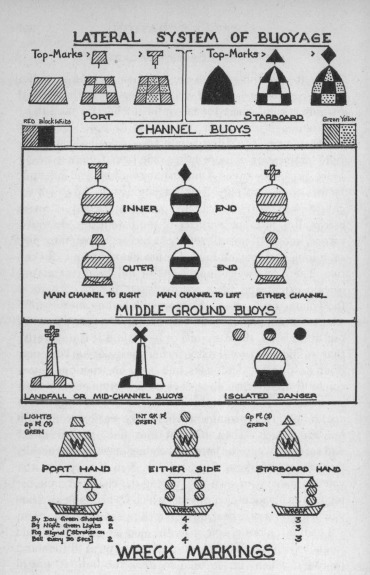

LATERAL SYSTEM OF BUOYAGE

Top-Marks >   >   Top-Marks > ▲   > ◆

PORT   STARBOARD

RED Black White   Green Yellow

CHANNEL BUOYS

INNER   END

OUTER   END

MAIN CHANNEL TO RIGHT   MAIN CHANNEL TO LEFT   EITHER CHANNEL

MIDDLE GROUND BUOYS

LANDFALL OR MID-CHANNEL BUOYS   ISOLATED DANGER

LIGHTS Gp Fl (3) GREEN   INT QK Fl GREEN   Gp Fl (3) GREEN

PORT HAND   EITHER SIDE   STARBOARD HAND

By Day Green Shapes   2   4   3
By Night Green Lights   2   4   3
Fog Signal [Strokes on   2   4   3
Bell every 30 Secs]

WRECK MARKINGS

Fig. 55

Changes in the Buoyage System

It is important to understand the buoyage system. Buoys mark navigable channels, wrecks, sandbanks, rocks, etc. and are identified by shape and colour by day, and by colour and flashing intervals at night. At present the system around the United Kingdom is based on the principle that a port hand buoy is left to port and a starboard hand buoy to starboard when going with the *main flood tide stream* (and vice-versa). This system is illustrated in Fig. 55. *However, it will be phased out* over a period of approximately four years beginning on 18 April 1977. It will be replaced in United Kingdom waters by the I.A.L.A. system 'A' (see Fig. 56). You will see at once by comparing the two systems that the I.A.L.A. system 'A' uses not only lateral marks but cardinal marks as well, and also isolated danger marks, safe water marks and other special marks. While the new I.A.L.A. system 'A' is being introduced, the direction of buoyage, instead of being related to the main flood tide direction, as previously, may be defined by either the general direction taken by the mariner *when approaching a harbour, etc. from seaward* or in some cases by the appropriate authority. As a general rule it will follow a clockwise direction around the land masses. The cardinal marks will be used to indicate that the deepest water in that area lies on the named side of the mark, to indicate the safe side on which to pass a danger, and to call attention to such things as bends, junctions, the end of a shoal, etc. With regard to lights for the lateral marks: Port hand (when fitted) will be Red (any rhythm) and Starboard hand Green (any rhythm). This new buoyage system follows years of discussion. Two systems have finally resulted: system 'A' (suitable for Europe, Africa, India, Australia and some Asian waters) is now agreed, and system 'B' is still being prepared. System 'A' uses a combination of two main types of mark, lateral and cardinal (see Fig. 56), as explained

IALA BUOYAGE SYSTEM 'A'

LATERAL MARKS

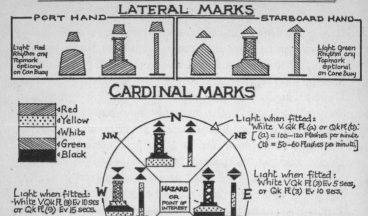

— PORT HAND —

Light Red
Rhythm any
Topmark
optional
on Can Buoy

STARBOARD HAND

Light Green
Rhythm any
Topmark
optional
on Cone Buoy

CARDINAL MARKS

◄ Red
◄ Yellow
◄ White
◄ Green
◄ Black

HAZARD OR POINT OF INTEREST

Light when fitted:
White V.Qk Fl (a) or Qk Fl (b).
[(a) = 100-120 Flashes per minute
(b) = 50-60 Flashes per minute]

Light when fitted:
White V Qk Fl (3) Ev 5 secs,
or Qk Fl (3) Ev 10 secs.

Light when fitted:
White VQk Fl (6) + long Flash (c)
Ev 10 secs or QFl (6) + long Flash
Ev 15 secs
[(c) = Not less than 2 secs duration.]

Light when fitted:
White VQk Fl (9) Ev 10 secs
or Qk Fl (9) Ev 15 secs.

ISOLATED DANGER MARKS

Light
when
fitted..
White
Gp Fl (2)

SAFE WATER MARKS

Lights
when fitted:
White Isophase
Occulting or
Long Flash
Ev 10 secs.

SPECIAL MARKS

[Topmarks, if any.]

Shape optional, but not conflicting with Navigational marks; eg: 'Can'
buoy not to be used in Starboard position. Light, when fitted, Yellow.

Fig. 56

above. The main things for the sailor to remember are:

a. Red = Port, or Left.

b. Green = Starboard, or Right.

c. The four buoys for North, South, East and West.

d. The marks for safe water, danger, direction and 'special'.

The new system is being introduced in stages, starting at the Greenwich Meridian in the English Channel and gradually spreading through Europe.

As soon as you are experienced enough to be making passages at sea I recommend a thorough study of the sections devoted to the buoyage system in an up-to-date copy of that invaluable book, *Reed's Nautical Almanac*, where all the information required is set out in detail. When you come to cruise you will need a nautical almanac, with its very full information about tides, lights, Collision Regulations and a hundred and one other things essential to the navigator. (*Reed's Nautical Almanac* also illustrates the limits of the areas where the new buoyage system will be phased in, and the approximate dates of the changes.)

When making a passage, keep a log-book (called a log). By entering the time, and the readings of the patent log, whenever course is altered, the distance run and any other relevant information, you will be able to 'work up the reckoning' and determine the ship's position with reasonable accuracy. If also it is found that, owing to having to make an alteration of course because of a shift of wind, the yacht is getting some way off her pre-arranged course, this will easily be seen on the chart by working up the reckoning, and a new course plotted to bring her to the ultimate destination. Always note the time whenever a bearing is taken, and never mark a bearing, estimated position, or fix on the chart, without putting the time down alongside. Always keep a log of all that is happening, and don't forget the golden rule: always know where you are.

INTERNATIONAL REGULATIONS FOR PREVENTING COLLISIONS AT SEA, 1972

The following are extracted from the above Regulations. I have omitted certain sections which are unlikely to affect the beginner in sail, so as not to make this part of the book too bulky.

PART A: GENERAL

Rule 1 Application

(a) These Rules shall apply to all vessels upon the high seas and in all waters connected therewith navigable by seagoing vessels.

(b) Nothing in these Rules shall interfere with the operation of special rules made by an appropriate authority for roadsteads, harbours, rivers, lakes or inland waterways connected with the high seas and navigable by seagoing vessels. Such special rules shall conform as closely as possible to these rules.

Rule 2 Responsibility

(a) Nothing in these Rules shall exonerate any vessel, or the owner, master or crew thereof, from the consequences of any neglect to comply with these Rules or of the neglect of any precaution which may be required by the ordinary practice of seamen, or by the special circumstances of the case.

(b) In construing and complying with these Rules due regard shall be had to all dangers of navigation and collision and to any special circumstances, including the limitations of the vessels involved, which may make a departure from these Rules necessary to avoid immediate danger.

Rule 3 General Definitions

For the purposes of these Rules, except where the context otherwise requires:

(a) The word 'vessel' includes every description of water craft, including non-displacement craft and seaplanes, used or capable of being used as a means of transportation on water.

(b) The term 'power-driven vessel' means any vessel propelled by machinery.

(c) The term 'sailing vessel' means any vessel under sail provided that propelling machinery, if fitted, is not being used.

(d) The term 'vessel engaged in fishing' means any vessel fishing with nets, lines, trawls or other fishing apparatus which restrict manoeuvrability, but does not include a vessel fishing with trolling lines or other fishing apparatus which do not restrict manoeuvrability.

(e) The word 'seaplane' includes any aircraft designed to manoeuvre on the water.

(f) The term 'vessel not under command' means a vessel which through some exceptional circumstance is unable to manoeuvre as required by these Rules and is therefore unable to keep out of the way of another vessel.

(g) The term 'vessel restricted in her ability to manoeuvre' means a vessel which from the nature of her work is restricted in her ability to manoeuvre as required by these Rules and is therefore unable to keep out of the way of another vessel.

(h) The term 'vessel constrained by her draught' means a power-driven vessel which because of her draught in relation to the available depth of water is severely restricted in her ability to deviate from the course she is following.

(i) The word 'underway' means that a vessel is not at anchor, or made fast to the shore, or aground.

(j) The words 'length' and 'breadth' of a vessel mean her length overall and greatest breadth.

(k) Vessels shall be deemed to be in sight of one another only when one can be observed visually from the other.

(l) The term 'restricted visibility' means any condition in which visibility is restricted by fog, mist, falling snow, heavy rainstorms, sandstorms or any other similar causes.

PART B: STEERING AND SAILING RULES
SECTION 1
Conduct of Vessels in any Condition of Visibility

Rule 4 Application
Rules in this Section apply in any condition of visibility.

Rule 7 Risk of Collision

(a) Every vessel shall use all available means appropriate to the prevailing circumstances and conditions to determine if risk of collision exists. If there is any doubt such risk shall be deemed to exist.

(d) In determining if risk of collision exists the following considerations shall be among those taken into account:

(i) such risk shall be deemed to exist if the compass bearing of an approaching vessel does not appreciably change;

(ii) such risk may sometimes exist even when an appreciable bearing change is evident, particularly when approaching a very large vessel or a tow or when approaching a vessel at close range.

Rule 8 Action to avoid Collision

(a) Any action taken to avoid collision shall, if the circumstances of the case admit, be positive, made in ample time and with due regard to the observance of good seamanship.

(b) Any alteration of course and/or speed to avoid collision shall, if the circumstances of the case admit, be large enough to be readily apparent to another vessel observing visually or by radar; a succession of small alterations of course and/or speed should be avoided.

Rule 9 Narrow Channels

(a) A vessel proceeding along the course of a narrow channel or fairway shall keep as near to the outer limit of the channel or fairway which lies on her starboard side as is safe and practicable.

(b) A vessel of less than 20 metres in length or a sailing vessel shall not impede the passage of a vessel which can safely navigate only within a narrow channel or fairway.

Rule 10 Traffic Separation Schemes

(j) A vessel of less than 20 metres in length or a sailing vessel shall not impede the safe passage of a power-driven vessel following a traffic lane.

SECTION II

Conduct of Vessels in Sight of One Another

Rule 11 Application
 Rules in this Section apply to vessels in sight of one another.

Rule 12 Sailing Vessels
 (a) when two sailing vessels are approaching one another, so as to involve risk of collision, one of them shall keep out of the way of the other as follows:

- (i) when each has the wind on a different side, the vessel which has the wind on the port side shall keep out of the way of the other;
- (ii) when both have the wind on the same side, the vessel which is to windward shall keep out of the way of the vessel which is to leeward;
- (iii) if a vessel with the wind on the port side sees a vessel to windward and cannot determine with certainty whether the other vessel has the wind on the port or on the starboard side, she shall keep out of the way of the other.

 (b) For the purposes of this Rule the windward side shall be deemed to be the side opposite to that on which the mainsail is carried or, in the case of a square-rigged vessel, the side opposite to that on which the largest fore-and-aft sail is carried.

Rule 13 Overtaking
 (a) Notwithstanding anything contained in the Rules of this Section any vessel overtaking any other shall keep out of the way of the vessel being overtaken.

 (b) A vessel shall be deemed to be overtaking when coming up with another vessel from a direction more than 22·5 degrees abaft her beam, that is, in such a position with reference to the vessel she is overtaking, that at night she would be able to see only the sternlight of that vessel but neither of her sidelights.

 (c) When a vessel is in any doubt as to whether she is overtaking another, she shall assume that this is the case and act accordingly.

(d) Any subsequent alteration of the bearing between the two vessels shall not make the overtaking vessel a crossing vessel within the meaning of these Rules or relieve her of the duty of keeping clear of the overtaken vessel until she is finally past and clear.

Rule 14 Head-on Situation

(a) When two power-driven vessels are meeting on reciprocal or nearly reciprocal courses so as to involve risk of collision each shall alter her course to starboard so that each shall pass on the port side of the other.

(b) Such a situation shall be deemed to exist when a vessel sees the other ahead or nearly ahead and by night she could see the masthead lights of the other in a line or nearly in a line and/or both sidelights and by day she observes the corresponding aspect of the other vessel.

(c) When a vessel is in any doubt as to whether such a situation exists she shall assume that it does exist and act accordingly.

Rule 15 Crossing Situation

When two power-driven vessels are crossing so as to involve risk of collision, the vessel which has the other on her own starboard side shall keep out of the way and shall, if the circumstances of the case admit, avoid crossing ahead of the other vessel.

Rule 16 Action by Give-way Vessel

Every vessel which is directed to keep out of the way of another vessel shall, so far as possible, take early and substantial action to keep well clear.

Rule 17 Action by Stand-on Vessel

(a) (i) Where one of two vessels is to keep out of the way the other shall keep her course and speed.

(ii) The latter vessel may however take action to avoid

collision by her manoeuvre alone, as soon as it becomes apparent to her that the vessel required to keep out of the way is not taking appropriate action in compliance with these Rules.

(b) When, from any cause, the vessel required to keep her course and speed finds herself so close that collision cannot be avoided by the action of the give-way vessel alone, she shall take such action as will best aid to avoid collision.

(c) A power-driven vessel which takes action in a crossing situation in accordance with sub-paragraph (a)(ii) of this Rule to avoid collision with another power-driven vessel shall, if the circumstances of the case admit, not alter course to port for a vessel on her own port side.

(d) This Rule does not relieve the give-way vessel of her obligation to keep out of the way.

Rule 18 Responsibilities between Vessels

Except where Rules 9, 10 and 13 otherwise require:

(a) A power-driven vessel underway shall keep out of the way of:

    (i) a vessel not under command;
    (ii) a vessel restricted in her ability to manoeuvre;
    (iii) a vessel engaged in fishing;
    (iv) a sailing vessel.

(b) A sailing vessel underway shall keep out of the way of:

    (i) a vessel not under command;
    (ii) a vessel restricted in her ability to manoeuvre;
    (iii) a vessel engaged in fishing.

(c) A vessel engaged in fishing when underway shall, so far as possible, keep out of the way of:

    (i) a vessel not under command;
    (ii) a vessel restricted in her ability to manoeuvre.

(d) (i) Any vessel other than a vessel not under command or a vessel restricted in her ability to manoeuvre shall, if the circumstances of the case admit, avoid impeding the safe passage of a vessel constrained by her draught, exhibiting the signals in Rule 28.

(ii) A vessel constrained by her draught shall navigate with
     particular caution having full regard to her special
     condition.

SECTION III
Conduct of Vessels in Restricted Visibility

Rule 19 Conduct of Vessels in Restricted Visibility

(a) This Rule applies to vessels not in sight of one another
when navigating in or near an area of restricted visibility.

(b) Every vessel shall proceed at a safe speed adapted to the
prevailing circumstances and conditions of restricted visibility.
A power-driven vessel shall have her engines ready for immediate
manoeuvre.

(c) Every vessel shall have due regard to the prevailing circumstances and conditions of restricted visibility when complying
with the Rules of Section I of this Part.

(e) Except where it has been determined that a risk of collision
does not exist, every vessel which hears apparently forward of
her beam the fog signal of another vessel, or which cannot avoid
a close-quarters situation with another vessel forward of her
beam, shall reduce her speed to the minimum at which she can
be kept on her course. She shall if necessary take all her way off
and in any event navigate with extreme caution until danger of
collision is over.

PART C: LIGHTS AND SHAPES

Rule 20 Application

(a) Rules in this Part shall be complied with in all weathers.

(b) The Rules concerning lights shall be complied with from
sunset to sunrise, and during such times no other lights shall be
exhibited, except such lights as cannot be mistaken for the lights
specified in these Rules or do not impair their visibility or
distinctive character, or interfere with the keeping of a proper
lookout.

(c) The lights prescribed by these Rules shall, if carried, also
be exhibited from sunrise to sunset in restricted visibility and
may be exhibited in all other circumstances when it is deemed
necessary.

(d) The Rules concerning shapes shall be complied with by day.

(e) The lights and shapes specified in these Rules shall comply with the provisions of Annex I to these Regulations.

Rule 21 Definitions

(a) 'Masthead light' means a white light placed over the fore and aft centreline of the vessel showing an unbroken light over an arc of the horizon of 225 degrees and so fixed as to show the light from right ahead to 22·5 degrees abaft the beam on either side of the vessel.

(b) 'Sidelights' means a green light on the starboard side and a red light on the port side each showing an unbroken light over an arc of the horizon of 112·5 degrees and so fixed as to show the light from right ahead to 22·5 degrees abaft the beam on its respective side. In a vessel of less than 20 metres in length the sidelights may be combined in one lantern carried on the fore and aft centre line of the vessel.

(c) 'Sternlight' means a white light placed as nearly as practicable at the stern showing an unbroken light over an arc of the horizon of 135 degrees and so fixed as to show the light 67·5 degrees from right aft on each side of the vessel.

(d) 'Towing light' means a yellow light having the same characteristics as the 'sternlight' defined in paragraph (c) of this Rule.

(e) 'All-round light' means a light showing an unbroken light over an arc of the horizon of 360 degrees.

(f) 'Flashing light' means a light flashing at regular intervals at a frequency of 120 flashes or more per minute.

Rule 22 Visibility of Lights

The lights prescribed in these Rules shall have an intensity as specified in Section 8 of Annex I to these Regulations so as to be visible at the following minimum ranges:

(b) In vessels of 12 metres or more in length but less than 50 metres in length:

- a masthead light, 5 miles; except that where the length of the vessel is less than 20 metres, 3 miles;
- a sidelight, 2 miles;

- a sternlight, 2 miles;
- a towing light, 2 miles;
- a white, red, green or yellow all-round light, 2 miles.

(c) In vessels of less than 12 metres in length:
- a masthead light, 2 miles;
- a sidelight, 1 mile;
- a sternlight, 2 miles;
- a towing light, 2 miles;
- a white, red, green or yellow all-round light, 2 miles.

Rule 23 Power-driven Vessels underway

(a) A power-driven vessel underway shall exhibit:
  (i) a masthead light forward;
  (ii) a second masthead light abaft of and higher than the forward one; except that a vessel of less than 50 metres in length shall not be obliged to exhibit such light but may do so;
  (iii) sidelights;
  (iv) a sternlight.

(b) An air-cushion vessel when operating in the non-displacement mode shall, in addition to the lights prescribed in paragraph (a) of this Rule, exhibit an all-round flashing yellow light.

(c) A power-driven vessel of less than 7 metres in length and whose maximum speed does not exceed 7 knots may, in lieu of the lights prescribed in paragraph (a) of this Rule, exhibit an all-round white light. Such vessel shall, if practicable, also exhibit sidelights.

Rule 24 Towing and Pushing

(a) A power-driven vessel when towing shall exhibit:
  (i) instead of the light prescribed in Rule 23(a)(i), two masthead lights forward in a vertical line. When the length of the tow, measuring from the stern of the towing vessel to the after end of the tow exceeds 200 metres, three such lights in a vertical line;
  (ii) sidelights;
  (iii) a sternlight;
  (iv) a towing light in a vertical line above the sternlight;

(v) when the length of the tow exceeds 200 metres, a diamond shape where it can best be seen.

(b) When a pushing vessel and a vessel being pushed ahead are rigidly connected in a composite unit they shall be regarded as a power-driven vessel and exhibit the lights prescribed in Rule 23.

(c) A power-driven vessel when pushing ahead or towing alongside, except in the case of a composite unit, shall exhibit:

(i) instead of the light prescribed in Rule 23(a)(i), two masthead lights forward in a vertical line;

(ii) sidelights;

(iii) a sternlight.

(d) A power-driven vessel to which paragraphs (a) and (c) of this Rule apply shall also comply with Rule 23(a)(ii).

(e) A vessel or object being towed shall exhibit:

(i) sidelights;

(ii) a sternlight;

(iii) when the length of the tow exceeds 200 metres, a diamond shape where it can best be seen.

Rule 25 Sailing Vessels underway and Vessels under Oars

(a) A sailing vessel underway shall exhibit:

(i) sidelights;

(ii) a sternlight.

(b) In a sailing vessel of less than 12 metres in length the lights prescribed in paragraph (a) of this Rule may be combined in one lantern carried at or near the top of the mast where it can best be seen.

(c) A sailing vessel underway may, in addition to the lights prescribed in paragraph (a) of this Rule, exhibit at or near the top of the mast, where they can best be seen, two all-round lights in a vertical line, the upper being red and the lower green, but these lights shall not be exhibited in conjunction with the combined lantern permitted by paragraph (b) of this Rule.

(d) (i) A sailing vessel of less than 7 metres in length shall, if practicable, exhibit the lights prescribed in paragraph (a) or (b) of this Rule, but if she does not, she shall have ready at hand an electric torch or lighted lantern showing a white light which shall be exhibited in sufficient time to prevent collision.

(ii) A vessel under oars may exhibit the lights prescribed in this Rule for sailing vessels, but if she does not, she shall have ready at hand an electric torch or lighted lantern showing a white light which shall be exhibited in sufficient time to prevent collision.

(e) A vessel proceeding under sail when also being propelled by machinery shall exhibit forward where it can best be seen a conical shape, apex downwards.

Rule 28 *Vessels constrained by their Draught*

A vessel constrained by her draught may, in addition to the lights prescribed for power-driven vessels in Rule 23, exhibit where they can best be seen three all-round red lights in a vertical line, or a cylinder.

Rule 30 *Anchored Vessels and Vessels aground*

(a) A vessel at anchor shall exhibit where it can best be seen:

(i) in the fore part, an all-round white light or one ball;

(ii) at or near the stern and at a lower level than the light prescribed in sub-paragraph (i), an all-round white light.

(b) A vessel of less than 50 metres in length may exhibit an all-round white light where it can best be seen instead of the lights prescribed in paragraph (a) of this Rule.

(c) A vessel at anchor may, and a vessel of 100 metres and more in length shall, also use the available working or equivalent lights to illuminate her decks.

(d) A vessel aground shall exhibit the lights prescribed in paragraph (a) or (b) of this Rule and in addition, where they can best be seen:

(i) two all-round red lights in a vertical line;

(ii) three balls in a vertical line.

(c) A vessel of less than 7 metres in length, when at anchor or aground, not in or near a narrow channel, fairway or anchorage, or where other vessels normally navigate, shall not be required to exhibit the lights or shapes prescribed in paragraphs (a), (b) or (d) of this Rule.

Part D: Sound and Light Signals

Rule 23 Definitions

(a) The word 'whistle' means any sound signalling appliance capable of producing the prescribed blasts and which complies with the specifications in Annex III to these Regulations.

(b) The term 'short blast' means a blast of about one second's duration.

(c) The term 'prolonged blast' means a blast of from four to six seconds' duration.

Rule 33 Equipment for Sound Signals

(a) A vessel of 12 metres or more in length shall be provided with a whistle and a bell and a vessel of 100 metres or more in length shall, in addition, be provided with a gong, the tone and sound of which cannot be confused with that of the bell. The whistle, bell and gong shall comply with the specifications in Annex III to these Regulations. The bell or gong or both may be replaced by other equipment having the same respective sound characteristics, provided that manual sounding of the required signals shall always be possible.

(b) A vessel of less than 12 metres in length shall not be obliged to carry the sound signalling appliances prescribed in paragraph (a) of this Rule but if she does not, she shall be provided with some other means of making an efficient sound signal.

Rule 34 Manoeuvring and Warning Signals

(a) When vessels are in sight of one another, a power-driven vessel underway, when manoeuvring as authorized or required by these Rules, shall indicate that manoeuvre by the following signals on her whistle:
- one short blast to mean 'I am altering my course to starboard';
- two short blasts to mean 'I am altering my course to port';

– three short blasts to mean 'I am operating astern propulsion'.

(b) Any vessel may supplement the whistle signals prescribed in paragraph (a) of this Rule by light signals, repeated as appropriate, whilst the manoeuvre is being carried out:

    (i) these light signals shall have the following significance:
- one flash to mean 'I am altering my course to starboard';
- two flashes to mean 'I am altering my course to port';
- three flashes to mean 'I am operating astern propulsion';

    (ii) the duration of each flash shall be about one second, the interval between flashes shall be about one second, and the interval between successive signals shall be not less than ten seconds.

    (iii) the light used for this signal shall, if fitted, be an all-round white light, visible at a minimum range of 5 miles, and shall comply with the provisions of Annex I.

(c) When in sight of one another in a narrow channel or fairway:

    (i) a vessel intending to overtake another shall in compliance with Rule 9 (e)(i) indicate her intention by the following signals on her whistle:
- two prolonged blasts followed by one short blast to mean 'I intend to overtake you on your starboard side';
- two prolonged blasts followed by two short blasts to mean 'I intend to overtake you on your port side';

    (ii) the vessel about to be overtaken when acting in accordance with Rule 9(e)(i) shall indicate her agreement by the following signal on her whistle:
- one prolonged, one short, one prolonged and one short blast, in that order.

(d) When vessels in sight of one another are approaching each other and from any cause either vessel fails to understand the intentions or actions of the other, or is in doubt whether sufficient action is being taken by the other to avoid collision, the vessel in doubt shall immediately indicate such doubt by giving at least five short and rapid blasts on the whistle. Such signal may be supplemented by a light signal of at least five short and rapid flashes.

(e) A vessel nearing a bend or an area of a channel or fairway where other vessels may be obscured by an intervening obstruction shall sound one prolonged blast. Such signal shall be answered with a prolonged blast by any approaching vessel that may be within hearing around the bend or behind the intervening obstruction.

(f) If whistles are fitted on a vessel at a distance apart of more than 100 metres, one whistle only shall be used for giving manoeuvring and warning signals.

Rule 35 Sound Signals in restricted Visibility

In or near an area of restricted visibility, whether by day or night, the signals prescribed in this Rule shall be used as follows:

(a) A power-driven vessel making way through the water shall sound at intervals of not more than 2 minutes one prolonged blast.

(b) A power-driven vessel underway but stopped and making no way through the water shall sound at intervals of not more than 2 minutes two prolonged blasts in succession with an interval of about 2 seconds between them.

(c) A vessel not under command, a vessel restricted in her ability to manoeuvre, a vessel constrained by her draught, a sailing vessel, a vessel engaged in fishing and a vessel engaged in towing or pushing another vessel shall, instead of the signals prescribed in paragraphs (a) or (b) of this Rule, sound at intervals of not more than 2 minutes three blasts in succession, namely one prolonged followed by two short blasts.

(d) A vessel towed or if more than one vessel is towed the last vessel of the tow, if manned, shall at intervals of not more than 2 minutes sound four blasts in succession, namely one prolonged followed by three short blasts. When practicable, this signal shall be made immediately after the signal made by the towing vessel.

(e) When a pushing vessel and a vessel being pushed ahead are rigidly connected in a composite unit they shall be regarded as a power-driven vessel and shall give the signals prescribed in paragraphs (a) or (b) of this Rule.

(f) A vessel at anchor shall at intervals of not more than one minute ring the bell rapidly for about 5 seconds. In a vessel of 100 metres or more in length the bell shall be sounded in the forepart of the vessel and immediately after the ringing of the bell the gong shall be sounded rapidly for about 5 seconds in the after part of the vessel. A vessel at anchor may in addition sound three blasts in succession, namely one short, one prolonged and one short blast, to give warning of her position and of the possibility of collision to an approaching vessel.

(g) A vessel aground shall give the bell signal and if required the gong signal prescribed in paragraph (f) of this Rule and shall, in addition, give three separate and distinct strokes on the bell immediately before and after the rapid ringing of the bell. A vessel aground may in addition sound an appropriate whistle signal.

(h) A vessel of less than 12 metres in length shall not be obliged to give the above-mentioned signals but, if she does not, shall make some other efficient sound signal at intervals of not more than 2 minutes.

(i) A pilot vessel when engaged on pilotage duty may in addition to the signals prescribed in paragraphs (a), (b) or (f) of this Rule sound an identity signal consisting of four short blasts.

PART E: EXEMPTIONS

Rule 38 Exemptions

Any vessel (or class of vessels) provided that she complies with the requirements of the International Regulations for Preventing Collisions at Sea, 1960, the keel of which is laid or which is at a corresponding stage of construction before the entry into force of these Regulations may be exempted from compliance therewith as follows:

(a) The installation of lights with ranges prescribed in Rule 22, until four years after the date of entry into force of these Regulations.

(b) The installation of lights with colour specifications as prescribed in Section 7 of Annex I to these Regulations, until four years after the date of entry into force of these Regulations.

(c) The repositioning of lights as a result of conversion from Imperial to metric units and rounding off measurement figures, permanent exemption.

(d) (i) The repositioning of masthead lights on vessels of less than 150 metres in length, resulting from the prescriptions of Section 3(a) of Annex I, permanent exemption.

(f) the repositioning of sidelights resulting from the prescriptions of Sections 2(g) and 3(b) of Annex I, until nine years after the date of entry into force of these Regulations.

(g) The requirements for sound signal appliances prescribed in Annex III, until nine years after the date of entry into force of these Regulations.

ANNEX I
Positioning and Technical Details of Lights and Shapes

1. Definition

The term 'height above the hull' means height above the uppermost continuous deck.

2. Vertical Positioning and Spacing of Lights

(b) The vertical separation of masthead lights of power-driven vessels shall be such that in all normal conditions of trim the after light will be seen over and separate from the forward light at a dis tance of 1,000 metres from the stem when viewed from sea level.

(c) The masthead light of a power-driven vessel of 12 metres but less than 20 metres in length shall be placed at a height above the gunwale of not less than 2·5 metres.

(d) A power-driven vessel of less than 12 metres in length may carry the uppermost light at a height of less than 2·5 metres above the gunwale. When however a masthead light is carried in addition to sidelights and a sternlight, then such masthead light shall be carried at least 1 metre higher than the sidelights.

(e) One of the two or three masthead lights prescribed for a power-driven vessel when engaged in towing or pushing another vessel shall be placed in the same position as the forward mast-head light of a power-driven vessel.

(f) In all circumstances the masthead light or lights shall be so placed as to be above and clear of all other lights and obstructions.

(g) The sidelights of a power-driven vessel shall be placed at a height above the hull not greater than three quarters of that of the forward masthead light. They shall not be so low as to be interfered with by deck lights.

(h) The sidelights, if in a combined lantern and carried on a power-driven vessel of less than 20 metres in length, shall be placed not less than 1 metre below the masthead light.

(i) When the Rules prescribe two or three lights to be carried in a vertical line, they shall be spaced as follows:

(ii) on a vessel of less than 20 metres in length such lights shall be spaced not less than 1 metre apart and the lowest of these lights shall, except where a towing light is required, not be less than 2 metres above the gunwale.

(iii) when three lights are carried they shall be equally spaced.

3. Horizontal Positioning and Spacing of Lights

(a) When two masthead lights are prescribed for a power-driven vessel, the horizontal distance between them shall not be less than one half of the length of the vessel but need not be more than 100 metres. The forward light shall be placed not more than one quarter of the length of the vessel from the stem.

5. Screens for Sidelights

The sidelights shall be fitted with inboard screens painted matt black, and meeting the requirements of Section 9 of this Annex. With a combined lantern, using a single vertical filament and a very narrow division between the green and red sections, external screens need not be fitted.

6. Shapes

(a) Shapes shall be black and of the following sizes:

(i) a ball shall have a diameter of not less than 0·6 metre;

(ii) a cone shall have a base diameter of not less than 0·6 metre and a height equal to its diameter;

    (iii) a cylinder shall have a diameter of at least 0·6 metre and a height of twice its diameter;

    (iv) a diamond shape shall consist of two cones as defined in (ii) above having a common base.

  (b) The vertical distance between shapes shall be at least 1·5 metres.

  (c) In a vessel of less than 20 metres in length shapes of lesser dimensions but commensurate with the size of the vessel may be used and the distance apart may be correspondingly reduced.

Sections 7, 8, 9, 10 and 11 of Annex I deal with lights in great detail, listing the required chromaticity and the intensity. I have (as in other instances) omitted this in what is after all a manual for people starting to sail; but it may easily be found in *Reed's Almanac*. The general effect is an increase in the power of navigation lights, and when you intend to make night passages you will have to take advice and make sure your navigation lights are adequately bright. A sailing yacht must have lights able to exhibit the required intensity at all angles from 5 degrees above to 5 degrees below the Horizontal (Paragraph 10(i)).

12. Manoeuvring Light

Notwithstanding the provisions of paragraph 2(f) of this Annex the manoeuvring light described in Rule 34(b) shall be placed in the same fore and aft vertical plane as the masthead light or lights and, where practicable, at a minimum height of 2 metres vertically above the forward masthead light, provided that it shall be carried not less than 2 metres vertically above or below the after masthead light. On a vessel where only one masthead light is carried the manoeuvring light, if fitted, shall be carried where it can best be seen, not less than 2 metres vertically apart from the masthead light.

13. Approval

The construction of lanterns and shapes and the installation of lanterns on board the vessel shall be to the satisfaction of the appropriate authority of the state where the vessel is registered.

BLOW, MY BULLY BOYS, BLOW!

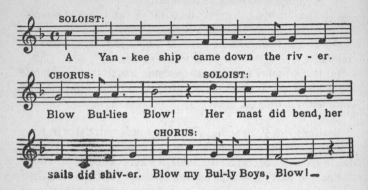

SOLOIST:

A Yan - kee ship came down the riv - er.

CHORUS: SOLOIST:

Blow Bul-lies Blow! Her mast did bend, her

CHORUS:

sails did shiv-er. Blow my Bul-ly Boys, Blow!

2. *Her sails were old, her sides were rotten,*
    Chorus: Blow, bullies, blow;
    Her charts her skipper had forgotten,
    Chorus: Blow, my bully boys, blow.

3. *And who d'ye think was skipper of her,*
    (Chorus as above).
    Why, Billy Haines is skipper of her,
    (Chorus as above).

4. *And how d'ye know he's skipper of her?*
    By the blood and guts that stream from her scupper.

5. *And who d'ye think is mate aboard her?*
    Santander James is mate aboard her.

6. *He'll make you wish you was dead and buried,*
    He'll make you wish he was dead and buried,

7. *He'll ride you down like you ride a spanker,*
    He'll ride you down like you ride a spanker.

8. *And who do you think is the second mate of her?*
    Why, some hard case what hates poor sailors.

9. *With Haines and the mate and a bucko greaser,*
   With Haines and the mate and a bucko greaser,

10. *You'll polish brass and you'll hog the cable,*
    You'll polish brass and you'll hog the cable,

11. *Oh, blow today and blow tomorrow,*
    Oh, blow away all grief and sorrow;

12. *So blow, my boys, and blow together;*
    Oh, blow, my boys, for better weather.

CHAPTER 17

Care of the Sails and Hull. Winter Storage and Fitting Out

—

GOOD-LOOKING sails add enormously to a yacht's appearance, and efficient sails make the whole difference to her performance. Take care of your sails. Keep them clean and dry. Do not walk on them or handle them with hands that have just been hauling in a muddy anchor chain.

When a sail-maker makes a sail, he puts roaches or curves along the edges. The luff, foot, and head are pulled straight when the sail is bent to the boom and hoisted, and being curved, they give a curvature to the sail that gives it the aerofoil shape necessary to make the boat sail to windward.

Never stow ship and turn in and allow the sails to dry out with a reef in. In a very small boat the sails can be unbent and taken ashore each night. In larger yachts where the mainsail is left bent on, see that it is properly furled and covered with a waterproof sail cover. A sail should be dry before it is furled. The best way to dry sails is by sailing on them. The next best way is to hoist them slackly at anchor. Thirdly, take them ashore and hang them over a clothes line in the sun or in a warm, dry attic. If you are drying sails at anchor, shake out all reefs first.

In recent years, there has been a great revolution in sail-making, and nowadays sails are made from synthetic fibres, Terylene, nylon, etc. These synthetic sails do not mildew and there is a tendency to stuff them into their sail bags wet, and any old how. They do not react well to such unkind treatment and emerge from their bags in a crumpled and creased state, and sometimes such creases are surprisingly hard to get rid of.

Proper sail maintenance is best left to the sailmakers. It is perfectly possible to do minor running repairs oneself, but at the end of the season it is usually wisest to send them to the sailmaker for washing, drying, and a thorough overhaul; and, if necessary, winter storage. When you are storing sails try and roll or fold them with as few creases as possible. Don't try and 'iron out' creases yourself!

Look after the hull too. It is often easy to tell a beginner by the appalling state of his craft. The hull can so easily and quickly be changed from a gleaming thing of beauty to a dirty, scarred object that can only discredit a ship in her owner's eyes and in the eyes of others. Now how does a hull get these scars?

Firstly, coming alongside other craft or wharfs. Always do this with care and always have plenty of fenders out. Secondly, other craft coming alongside you. Always have fenders out on your vacant side. Another craft may come alongside at any time and is quite likely to harm you unless you are properly fended. It is no good arguing that it is the other chap's responsibility. A streak of black paint on your white topsides does not entitle you to demand that the owner of the vessel who caused it should repaint your yacht; it was naturally unintentional and an accident, but it looks horrible.

Thirdly, watch out for the dinghy! Have a good thick rope or rubber strip all round as a fender and always take care when bringing the dinghy alongside.

Fourthly, the anchor is a bad offender. When you weigh, wash off the mud before bringing the anchor aboard and be careful that you do not give the bow a jab with one of the flukes as you haul it up. Lash it down when it is secured on deck to prevent it moving around when the ship's movement is lively.

Look out for dry rot. This is a danger to all wooden craft. It is a germ disease, being a fungus that spreads rapidly and destroys the wood. To keep it away from your craft there are two protective measures – paint and ventilation. Always keep all wood covered with sufficient coats of paint or varnish, which must be put on when the wood is completely dry. Always give the boat adequate ventilation. Let the sun and air get inside her. Examine the cabin and the hull to see that there are no places where stale air can collect. The current of air in a ship, no matter which way the wind is, is from aft forward. See that air can flow through the ship and ventilate all the corners.

Once dry rot has started there is one thing and one thing only that you must do. Practise immediate and ruthless surgery. Get out not only the affected wood but any wood round it that may be affected. Get expert advice on this and act *at once*. When new wood is put in to replace what was removed, make sure it has been properly seasoned. Get a job of this sort (and in fact a job of any sort) done by a *reliable firm of yacht builders*. There are too many crooks about these days, sullying a noble and delightful trade by turning out bad workmanship and using rotten materials. Such people, who send the unwary to sea in rotten and badly-found craft, are plain murderers.

Worms are another cause of hull trouble. The gribble worm is the most common in the British Isles. The teredo is worse, but he likes warmth and abounds mainly in tropical waters. Worms bore into and eat wood. Antifouling paint keeps them at bay. Have a good antifouling. The International Paint Company produce a good one. Worms usually get a start in the rudder trunk (and the centreboard case in centreboard boats) where the antifouling can't get easily. Try to get the antifouling into these places. It can be done. Putting copper sheeting on the bottom is one answer to worms and marine growth on the bottom. It is expensive, but advisable for a vessel likely to be much in the Mediterranean or tropical waters. You can do it yourself, but it is a long job; using copper paint is an easier method and, according to some, just as effective. If your hull is made of reinforced plastic, of course, worms and rot may do their worst! (See Chapter 3.) Finally, wash the topsides down with fresh water reasonably often. The salt deposit takes away the glow and sheen of enamel paint, and only fresh water will get the salt off.

When you lay up for the winter, lay up with a good yard. It is worth the extra money. They will see that the boat is in a dry shed or has an adequate waterproof cover, properly ventilated. They will also see that she is properly 'cradled'. That is to say that the yacht is supported firmly at several points along the bottom and is securely lashed in position. A boat which is supported only at the ends will sag in the centre, and vice versa. The former is called sagging; the latter, hogging. They are the same as the alternate hogging and sagging strains borne by a ship riding over successive waves at sea, but in the case of bad cradling, the strain is both continuous and completely unnecessary.

If your yacht has a cabin, the hatch and portholes should be left open, and also all lockers and interior doors. Floor boards should be taken up and all ballast removed and the bilges thoroughly cleaned out. The ballast should be stowed away where it is dry. The mast should be unstepped and placed in a shed, supported, like the hull, at a sufficient number of places to keep it from bending. All wire rigging should be removed, examined, and thoroughly greased before storage. All running rigging and blocks should be removed and the blocks cleaned and the pins and sheaves removed, greased, and put back. Everything that is removable should be not only removed and stored but *labelled*. Make out an inventory, give the yard one copy and keep the other. The sails should be washed in fresh water, thoroughly dried, and stored. A good sail-makers' will do this for you for a moderate charge, better than you can yourself. Have a fire insurance on the boat during winter storage. Most policies include this. Insurance firms generally quote three three types of policy. Full racing and/or cruising, (2) laid up afloat or in a mud berth, and (3) laid up ashore. Always have a good insurance policy on the boat.

Visit your boat occasionally in the winter and see that nothing has happened to her – but then if you've got sea fever, the difficulty is far more likely to be to keep away from her – and come to that, why should you?

If you do not have your yacht hauled out of the water altogether, you can keep her in what is called a mud berth, that is a berth in which the yacht makes her own little hole in the mud in which she sits at low water, and is only afloat at high water. Some people say that this method of laying up, by keeping the hull wet, keeps it cooler in the hot periods that come sometimes in the early spring and so prevents the seams opening through the heat. If you do have your boat in a mud berth, avoid crowded yacht yards where the yachts in mud berths are very close to each other. If there is a strong wind at high tide they will bump against one another and do damage unless they are thoroughly fended off with outsize fenders. If the yard of your choice wishes to lay your yacht up in this manner and there is no alternative, see that she is securely moored and thoroughly well fended.

And then at last when spring really comes and you begin to put into action all the fireside dreams and plans of the winter, there comes the exciting and most important job of fitting out. To begin with, inspect everything thoroughly. Examine the boat very carefully for rot and worms. The hull (the centreboard and rudder trunk, the dead wood and rudder post, and the garboards, in particular). Inspect all seams to see if they have opened up, and examine the butt ends of the planks to see if they have 'sprung' at all and need refastening. You will have to decide whether you can afford to get the yard to do all your fitting out or some of it, I would, with deference, suggest the following as a good principle. There are some jobs which in my opinion it is wisest to get the yard to do. Examining the hull. Any recaulking, paying, or recanvasing decks. Stepping the mast. Putting on the antifouling (not necessarily the antifouling priming) and launching. After a season or so, G.R.P. hulls will need painting too (also decks). But there is, on the whole, less work with G.R.P. (see my remarks later in this chapter). Much depends on two things – time and money. Most people's time is so short that they do not want all their available holiday time occupied in fitting out. The following advice is for those who will be doing their own painting and varnishing and letting the yard do the rest, including setting up the standing rigging and reeving the halliards, runners, and main sheet. This, for a reasonably busy man, is a good arrangement. Painting takes time, and, by doing your own, you will save a lot of money in man-hours. On the other hand the yard will have a reasonable amount of employment from your yacht, which is only fair, if they have housed you all winter. By doing the painting and varnishing you will be making an important contribution to the yacht's welfare and appearance and you will derive real satisfaction from the work involved, and it *is* hard work to do it properly. Some yards do not allow the owner to do any work on his own yacht if they house her. I have never met one of these, but I am told they exist. You must find out when asking for terms for laying up.

It is a good plan to let the yard go over the hull for you and examine it carefully. When you buy the yacht your surveyor will have the keel bolts tested, so there is normally no need for this, but if you are in any doubt get the yard to knock them out and see what sort of condition they are in. Stepping the mast is much more easily done by the yard, and it is best, if you can afford it, to let them set up the standing rigging, as the two jobs go hand in hand. Reeving running rigging can be done by you if you wish. Personally I do mine. Putting the antifouling undercoat and antifouling on the bottom can be done by you, but it is very hard work. Antifouling paint is thick and tacky and rather wearisome to put on. It is a trick amongst some unscrupulous workmen to thin it down with spirit. This makes the task of putting it on much easier but it nullifies most if not all of the antifouling properties of the paint, thereby wasting your money. If you can afford to let the yard put on the antifouling I should do so. You can, if you wish, put on the undercoat of priming yourself. A boat whose bottom has been painted with antifouling paint used to be launched within 24 hours. With these types of antifouling the final coat must be put on within 24 hours of the time of launching. This is easy enough for a yard to organize, but in fact nowadays the question of timing has been greatly simplified for there are antifoulings on the market (a very good one is T.B.T., made by International Yacht Paints) which can stand being out of water for up to six weeks before launching.

Assuming then that you are going to paint, let us consider what you will have to do. The first thing to do is to decide whether the topsides are to be burnt off and painted, or washed, rubbed down, and painted. If the paint is old and many layers have accumulated with the years it would be advisable to burn off. Similarly, if the colour of the last coat is say red or blue and you wish to change to white – burn off. Every scratch will show otherwise. But do not burn off unless it is really necessary. It is a very long job, and unless you have great determination and patience let the yard do it. The following is the procedure to follow when painting. It may seem over-particular, but it is worth it. The secret of a well-painted and gleaming hull is in the preparation and working up rather than in the final coat.

1. *If the topsides have to be burnt off.*
   (a) Mark in the boot top with tacks.
   (b) Burn off the topsides. Hold blow lamp in left hand and
        scraper in right. Work from the right to the left always.
        The paint should be scorched so that it comes off easily.
        Be careful not to burn the wood.
   (c) Rub down with sandpaper.
   (d) Rake out any loose stopping in the seams.
   (e) Give a coat of white lead paint.
   (f) Stop in seams where loose stopping was removed.
   (g) Rub down with sandpaper.
   (h) Give a coat of white lead paint.
   (i) Rub down with sandpaper.
   (j) Give one coat of undercoating. (Supplied by the firm
        from whom you have bought the final enamel coat.)
   (k) Rub down.
   (l) Give one coat of undercoating.
   (m) Rub down more lightly.
   (n) Give final enamel coat.

2. *If the topsides do not have to be burnt off.*
   (a) Wash topsides down.
   (b) Remove any loose stopping.
   (c) Rub down with sandpaper or water sandpaper and dry
        afterwards with washleather.
   (d) Spot paint bare patches to bring whole surface level.
   (e) Give one coat of undercoating.
   (f) Stop in where stopping was removed.
   (g) Rub down.
   (h) Give one coat of undercoating.
   (i) Rub down more lightly.
   (j) Give final enamel coat.

When choosing a colour remember that white keeps the
sides cool, looks very smart, wears well, and does not show
salt water stains. On the other hand, it shows every other
mark. Black attracts and retains heat, shows salt stains, and
needs frequent washing down with fresh water in conse-

quence. A dark painted yacht always appears small, but at the same time looks a thoroughbred. White gives an illusion of size.

If your boat is constructed of plywood, you should treat it as if it were ordinary wood, but remember that it is very absorbent sometimes, in which case a coat of priming mixed with 6 per cent white spirit should be used. If your boat is of resin/fibreglass construction, and it is desirable to paint it, you simply need to give one undercoat and one top coat of enamel. If the enamel is in bad condition you should first remove it with sandpaper, or 'Pintoff' and scraper, and then apply two undercoats and one of enamel. Remember that all fibreglass must be roughened before painting.

If your boat has a steel hull, before painting be sure it is completely free from rust, dirt, and grease. The hull should be primed before painting. The International Paint Company's 'Bare Plate' Primer is good for this.

VARNISHING

Once again, it is the preparation that counts. If the wood under the varnish has become stained, you must use varnish remover and a scraper and scrape right down to bare wood. Otherwise you need only rub it down.

1. *If it is necessary to scrape off.*
    (a) Apply the varnish remover, using a brush. Work only a small area at a time. Let the varnish remover stand for four or five minutes before starting to scrape.
    (b) Wash down with turpentine.
    (c) Bleach any black spots in the wood with a strong solution of bleaching acid.
    (d) Rub down with sandpaper.
    (e) Give one coat of varnish.
    (f) Rub down with sandpaper.
    (g) Give one coat of varnish.

(h)	Rub down lightly.
(i)	Give one coat of varnish.

It is a good idea when varnishing bare wood to fill the grain first with transparent grain filler, smeared on and then rubbed down. This makes a nice smooth base for the varnish.

2.	*If it is not necessary to scrape off.*
(a)	Wash well.
(b)	Rub down with sandpaper.

Then as above, giving two or more coats as desired. Always varnish on a fine dry day when there is not much wind. Varnish *before* painting the topsides, otherwise the dirt when you wash down will be washed over them. If you follow these instructions your brightwork and topsides will look smart and will last well.

The old natural copal varnishes have been virtually replaced by the new synthetic varnishes. Polyurethane paints and varnishes are now extensively used, and very good they are. They dry very quickly and in consequence it is best to use a large brush and work a small area at a time, always in the same direction. Remember when changing to a polyurethane paint or varnish you must first get back to bare wood. If applied over a conventional coating there is a risk that a polyurethane will not adhere properly, will not be water-resistant and will break down soon. Follow carefully the instructions given by the makers.

With which piece of basically sound advice, I bring this latest edition of the book to a close. Good sailing!

'Can't understand these uncivil-
ized fellows who go out of sight
of land and sleep on board
and don't wash and
all that!'